50 BEST ROUTES
on
Scottish Mountains
RALPH STORER

To my mother and father
who also loved the mountains

A DAVID & CHARLES BOOK

First published 1987 as 100 Best Routes on Scottish Mountains
Reprinted 1988, 1989, 1991, 1996
This edition 1994
Paperback edition 1998

ISBN 0 7153 0637 5

Designed and produced by Cooling Brown, Hampton, Middlesex
Edited by Clare Hill
Printed in Italy by Milanostampa SpA
for David & Charles
Brunel House Newton Abbot Devon

THE AUTHOR

Ralph Storer is an experienced and respected climber, walker and mountain biker who has pursued his chosen sports at the highest level. Currently a lecturer in computer studies at Napier University, Edinburgh, one of his great passions is for outdoor activities and the Scottish countryside. He writes regularly for mountaineering and walking magazines and is also the author of *Exploring Scottish Hill Tracks, 50 More Routes on Scottish Mountains, 50 Best Routes on Skye and Raasay* and *50 Classic Routes on Scottish Mountains*, also published by David & Charles.

ACKNOWLEDGEMENTS

A book of this nature could not have been written without many years of experience on Scottish mountains or without the companionship of those who have accompanied me on the hill during these years. It would take too long and perhaps be inappropriate to thank all the companions who have climbed with me and aided, wittingly or unwittingly, in the writing of this book, for climbing forges bonds that need never be stated and can never be broken. I am grateful to all of them for the many hours spent in their company.

There are others without whose specific help this book could not have reached fruition. Donald MacDonald's advice on Gaelic was invaluable, although the phonetic interpretation of Gaelic pronunciation is my sole responsibility. Don Sargeant provided the sketch maps and Jo Crompton, Wendy Gibson and Sue Horsburgh provided transport and support during sometimes hectic days on the hill. I thank them all.

■ All photographs by the author except route 17 (Dave Long) and route 33 (Ian Chuter). Cover photographs: (*front*) The Crianlarich and Tyndrum hills from Beinn Achaladair: (*back*) The view across Loch Etive from Ben Cruachan (author)

CONTENTS

Preface to the Second Edition

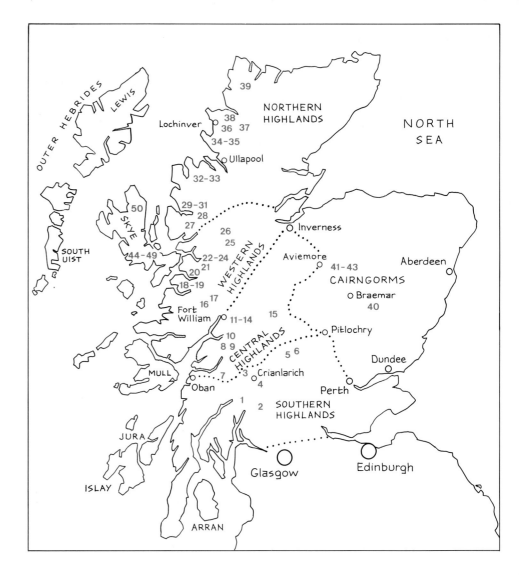

The second, all-colour, two-volume edition of *100 Best Routes on Scottish Mountains* follows seven years on from the first edition and incorporates a number of changes. Obvious and necessary updates include new paths up The Cobbler (route 1) and The Storr (route 50), a new Land Rover track up Srath Dionard (route 39) and new starting points for Ben Alder (route 15) and Sgurr na Ciche (route 17), owing to gates that now restrict car access to the old starting points. The new format has also enabled more detailed route descriptions to be given in many cases, and in a few cases route grids have been updated to reflect changes on the ground over the years. Many thanks to all readers who have written with suggestions.

The division of the 100 routes into two volumes of 50 has been done mainly on a geographical basis, to provide a cross-section of Highland hillwalking in each volume; the Islands section only has been divided on the basis of access, all Skye routes appearing in volume one (*50 Best Routes*) and all other island routes in volume two (*50 More Routes*). One route (Luinne Bheinn, route 19) has been reduced in length to make it more manageable, without losing any of its character.

I hope the routes presented in this book provide the reader with as much joy as they have the author.

INTRODUCTION

The mountain walker in Scotland is spoilt for choice. In the Highlands there are 284 Munros (separate mountains over 3,000ft/914m), a further 227 Tops over 3,000ft/914m, 221 Corbetts (separate mountains over 2,500ft/762m) and countless lesser heights – enough to last a lifetime and more. The volumes in the *Best Routes* series contain a personal choice of the best walking and scrambling routes in this mountain playground, from short afternoon rambles to day-long expeditions, from roadside summits to remote mountain sanctuaries, from gentle paths to kneebreakingly-steep hillsides, from hands-in-pockets-whistle-while-you-walk strolls to thrilling scrambles.

Any book of this nature begs the question 'What constitutes *best*?', for beauty lies in the eye of the beholder. Some walkers may prefer the vast windswept plateaus of the Cairngorms in winter, others the sharp peaks of Skye on a long summer gloaming. The routes chosen are those I have found to be most enjoyable, would most want to repeat and would most recommend, given the following constraints:

1 A route must ascend a mountain over 2,000ft/610m. The fascination with Munros has for too long led to the neglect of some superb smaller mountains; of the 50 routes in this volume, 7 are on mountains under 3,000ft/914m.

2 A route must contain no rock climbing (ie on which a rope would normally be required).

This does not exclude some scrambles on which walkers of a nervous disposition would never venture – even with a safety net.

3 A route must start from a place that can be reached by motorised transport (plus a ferry if necessary), and end at the same place. There are too many guidebooks whose routes begin in the middle of nowhere and end somewhere else in the middle of nowhere.

4 A route must be able to be completed by walkers of reasonable fitness in a single day. This does not exclude some routes whose completion may be impracticable in daylight in the winter.

5 The overall list of routes must represent a cross-section of all the Highland regions. Fifty routes in Skye, no matter how attractive, would be unsuitable for a guidebook to the best of Scotland.

The list of suggested routes has already provoked many hours of heated debate among colleagues – yet the amount of agreement is surprising, so much so that I would venture to say that most experienced Scottish walkers would agree with the vast majority of mountains chosen (if not the exact routes). I hope that the following pages will help while away many a pleasant hour in planning, anticipation and reflection.

ROUTES
The 50 routes are divided into six regions in accordance with accepted geographical divisions and common usage:
- The Southern Highlands: 6 routes – Routes 1-6
- The Central Highlands: 9 routes – Routes 7-15
- The Western Highlands: 11 routes – Routes 16-26
- The Northern Highlands: 13 routes – Routes 27-39
- The Cairngorms: 4 routes – Routes 40-43
- The Islands: 7 routes – Routes 44-50

Within each region routes are listed in approximately south-to-north, west-to-east order.

SKETCH MAPS
Sketch maps show each route's major features but are not intended for use on the hill. 1:50,000 scale OS maps are the most suitable for most Scottish mountain walking, but the OS 1:25,000 Outdoor Leisure maps to the Cuillin and Torridon Hills and the High Tops of the Cairngorms are recommended for these more complex areas. Beside each sketch map is indicated the number of the OS 1:50,000 map on which the route appears and the grid reference of the route's starting point (eg route 32 – OS: 19, GR: 114850). Some routes overlap two OS maps (eg route 31 – OS: 19/25) and others may appear on either of two maps (eg route 17 – OS: 33 or 40).

MAP SYMBOLS

▲ Munro
△ Top (in Munro's Tables)
● Other summit over 3000'/914 m
○ Summit over 2500'/762 m
■ Summit over 2000'/610 m
□ Summit under 2000'/610 m

⊔⊔⊔⊔ Cliff

⌇⌇ River

⊣⊢ Waterfall

Route

– – – Other paths, tracks, forest roads, etc.

═══ Road (public or accessible to public)

+++++ Railway

+++●+++ Railway Station

■ Building

Freshwater Loch

Sea/Sea Loch

The classification of mountains as Munros or Tops is based on the 1997 edition of Munro's Tables, incorporating revisions made since the 1891 publication of Sir Hugh Munro's original list, which contained 283 Munros and a further 255 Tops. Many walkers (including the author) regret any tampering with Sir Hugh's list, apart from reclassification following revision of heights on the map, but the latest edition is the *de facto* arbiter of the Tables. There are no clear criteria of what makes a mountain a Munro, a Top or neither, beyond the definition of a Munro as a separate mountain over 3,000ft/914m and a Top as a subsidiary summit over 3,000ft/914m.

MEASUREMENTS
Route distances are specified in both miles (to the nearest half-mile) and kilometres (to the nearest kilometre); short distances in the text are specified in metres (an approximate imperial measurement is yards).

Mountain heights are specified in metres and feet. Metric heights have been obtained from OS 2nd Series 1:50,000 maps. Equivalent heights in feet have been obtained by multiplying the height in metres by 3.28 (rounded down); these may not tally with heights on old OS one-inch-to-the-mile maps, which were obtained from an earlier survey.

The total amount of ascent for the whole route is specified to the nearest 10m (50ft). This is an approximation based on OS map heights and contours, which are shown at 10m inter-

vals and are in many instances omitted because of cartographic complexity.

Route times (to the nearest half-hour) are based on the time it should take a person of reasonable fitness to complete the route in good summer conditions. They take into account length of route, amount of ascent, technical difficulty, type of terrain and short stoppages, but do not make allowances for long stoppages and adverse weather. They are roughly standard between routes for comparison purposes and can be adjusted where necessary by a factor appropriate to the individual.

In winter, routes will normally take much longer, depending on conditions. A pre-dawn start is often necessary and some of the longer routes are best tackled as two-day expeditions, camping en route or making use of a bothy (useful bothies are noted in the text).

MOUNTAIN NAMES
Most Highland names are Gaelic in origin and the ability to pronounce and understand Gaelic names can add much to the pleasure of walking in Scotland. To this end a guide to the meaning of all mountain names is given in the Glossary/Index *(p110)* and a guide to pronunciation is given below.

The production of such a guide is made difficult by a number of factors. OS maps, despite their otherwise excellence, appear to have been named by Sassenachs, for they abound in Gaelic misspellings, misunderstandings, misuses and misplacements. It is with some misgivings that the author has retained OS spellings for the purpose of standardisation. Some OS misspellings make pronunciation impossible. Stob Diamh (route 7), for instance, is a misspelling of either Damh (stag) or Daimh (the genitive of Damh); any attempt at a direct pronunciation would be ludicrous. In addition, some names have become anglicised to such an extent that it would be pedantic to enforce a purist pronunciation on a non-Gaelic speaker. For example, the correct pronunciation of Ben is something akin to Pane, with a soft *n* as in the first syllable of *onion*. Moreover, pronunciation differs, sometimes markedly, throughout the Highlands and Islands.

Despite these problems, the phonetic guide given below and shown in the Glossary should enable a good attempt at a pronunciation that would be intelligible to a Gaelic speaker:

Y before a vowel pronounced as in *you*
OW pronounced as in *town*
CH pronounced as in Scottish *loch* or
  German *noch*
TCH pronounced as *ch* in *church*
Œ pronounced as in French *oeuf* or the
  u in *turn*

Toponomy (the study of place name meanings) is complicated by OS misspellings, changes in spelling and word usage over the centuries, words with more than one meaning and unknown origin of names (Gaelic, Norse, Irish etc). For example, consider the origin of the names Ben Nevis (see route 13) and Cuillin (see route 44). Meanings given in this book are the most commonly accepted, even if disputed; when the meaning is doubtful it is annotated with poss (i.e. possible); some names are too obscure to be given any meaning.

ASSESSMENT AND SEASONAL NOTES

The assessment is intended as a brief overview of the nature of the route during summer conditions. Under snow, Scottish mountains become much more serious propositions. Paths are obliterated, grassy hillsides become treacherous slopes, ridges become corniced, stone shoots become snow gullies, walking becomes more difficult and tiring, terrain becomes featureless in adverse weather, and white-outs and spindrift reduce visibility to zero.

Winter conditions vary from British to Alpine to Arctic from November through to April, though sometimes earlier and later and varying from locality to locality – it is possible to encounter hard snow and ice even in October and May.

It cannot be stressed enough that no-one should venture into the Scottish mountains in winter without adequate clothing, an ice-axe and experience (or the company of an experienced person). In hard winter conditions crampons will also be required.

The number of accidents – many of them fatal – which have occurred in Scotland over the last few winters should leave no-one in doubt as to the need for caution.

Many of the routes in this book become major mountaineering expeditions in winter and should not be attempted by walkers; such routes are indicated in Seasonal Notes. The viability of other routes in winter depends on grade and conditions; in general the higher the summer grade, the higher the winter grade. Note, however, that even a normally straightforward winter route may be subject to avalanche or hard ice, to say nothing of potentially life-threatening, severe winter weather.

The Scottish mountains in winter have an Alpine attraction and reward the prepared walker with unforgettable experiences, but if in doubt stay off the hill. Bearing these points in mind, the seasonal notes for each route indicate any specific places where particular difficulties are normally likely to be encountered, thus enabling the walker to be better prepared. Where an easier escape route presents itself this also is noted.

ROUTE DIFFICULTY

The overall difficulty of each route is shown in the form of a grid, as explained on page 9. It will be apparent from this grading system that not all the routes in this book are for novices. Many accidents in the Scottish hills are caused by walkers attempting routes outside their capabilities, and the grading system is intended to enable a more realistic route appraisal. On the more technically difficult routes, easier alternatives are noted in the text or in the seasonal notes, if applicable.

ACCESS

Any access restrictions on the routes are noted in the text, apart from stalking restrictions. Whatever one's ethical stance on deer stalking, the fact remains that most of the Scottish Highlands is privately owned, and non-compliance with stalking restrictions is likely to be counter-productive and may well lead to the imposition of further restrictions. In addition, if estate revenue is lost because of interference with stalking activities, the alternative may be afforestation or worse – which would not only increase access problems but could irreparably alter the landscape.

The stalking season for stags runs normally from mid-August to mid-October, but varies from locality to locality. Access notices dot the roadside and information on stalking activities can be obtained from estate offices and head stalkers. For a complete list of access restrictions and estate addresses see *Access for Mountaineers and Hillwalkers*, which is published jointly by the Mountaineering Council of Scotland and the Scottish Landowners' Federation.

Land shown on the OS map as belonging to public bodies such as the National Trust for Scotland and the Nature Conservancy Council is normally not subject to access restrictions.

Finally, it should be noted that all river directions given in the text as 'left bank' and 'right bank', in accordance with common usage, refer to the direction you will be pointing towards when facing downstream.

GRID

	1	2	3	4	5
grade					
terrain					
navigation					
seriousness					

An at-a-glance grid for each route indicates the route's over-all difficulty, where difficulty consists not only of **grade** (i.e. technical difficulty) but also type of **terrain** (irrespective of grade), difficulty of **navigation** with a compass in adverse weather, and **seriousness** (i.e. difficulty of escape in case of curtailment of route for one reason or another. This is based upon a criteria of length and restricted line of escape). These factors vary over the duration of the route and should not be taken as absolute, but they do provide a useful general guide and enable comparisons to be made between routes. Each category is graded, ranging from 1 (easiest) to 5 (hardest)

Grade

1 Mostly not too steep
2 Appreciable steep sections
3 Some handwork required
4 Easy scramble
5 Hard scramble

Terrain

1 Excellent, often on paths
2 Good
3 Reasonable
4 Rough
5 Tough

Navigation

1 Straightforward
2 Reasonably straightforward
3 Appreciable accuracy required
4 Hard
5 Extremely hard

Seriousness

1 Straightforward escape
2 Reasonably straightforward escape
3 Appreciable seriousness
4 Serious
5 Very serious

Meall Garbh (Route 5, page 18).

	1	2	3	4	5
grade					
terrain					
navigation					
seriousness					

OS MAP: 56
GR: 294049
DISTANCE: 5½ miles (9km)
ASCENT: 900m (2,950ft)
TIME: 6 hours

ASSESSMENT: a route of sharp scrambles and surprises on a remarkable Southern Highland peak.

SEASONAL NOTES: in winter conditions care is required when climbing the slopes to the summit ridge and the ascent of the summit rocks of the south and central peaks, though beautiful when iced, may be impracticable.

'There must be something magnetic about The Cobbler. Many times I have gone to Arrochar alone, meaning to climb Ben Vane, the Brack or one of the other tops, but early afternoon would find me nearing the summit of The Cobbler.'

BEN HUMBLE (*On Scottish Hills*, 1946)

The great rock peak of The Cobbler, looking like a cobbler bent over his last, dominates the approach to Arrochar from Loch Lomond. It is the most striking mountain in the Southern Highlands and by far the most spectacular of all the Arrochar Alps yet, because it fails to reach the magic '3,000ft' (914m) mark, it is often ignored in favour of neighbouring Munros of less character. In such ways does the Munro bagger miss the best of the Highlands, for the ascent of The Cobbler's three bold, rocky tops involves some exhilarating scrambling, and the main summit has a surprising sting in the tail.

Begin at a lay-by on the A83, immediately south of the Succoth turn-off west of Arrochar. At the far end of the lay-by an obvious path enters the woods, climbs steeply to the foot of some crags, then turns sharp left to take a level route across the hillside to the Allt a' Bhalachain. Beyond a dam, the path follows the left bank (right side) of the burn to the Narnain Boulders, two large rocks that have yielded climbs, and a howff (shelter). A few hundred metres further on, the path crosses the burn and heads up into the corrie beneath the

Map labels: BEN NARNAIN · THE COBBLER 884m/2900' · Allt Sugach · Allt a' Bhalachain · Succoth · A 83 · Glen Croe · Croe Water · Arrochar · Loch Long · A 814 · kilometre · mile

three peaks. The centre peak is the highest; the south (left-hand) peak is known as the Cobbler's Wife; the north (right-hand) peak is known as the Cobbler's Last. The north peak features impressive overhangs which look quite daunting, but is in fact the easiest of the three peaks to ascend.

Follow the well-worn path up to the bealach between the centre and north peaks, making a detour, if so inclined, to search for The Cobbler Cave at the foot of the obvious Ramshead Ridge beneath the north peak. Once onto the plateau, turn right to follow the broad ridge to the north summit rocks. The impressive view over the edge is not recommended to those who suffer from heights.

Return to the bealach and walk up to the main peak. The summit block is a short exposed scramble that has turned back many a walker. It involves crawling through a rock window ('Argyll's Eyeglass') and climbing a couple of airy sloping ledges to the flat roof. Legend has it that every Campbell chief had to prove his manhood by gaining the top.

The traverse to the south peak is another good, but harder, scramble that many walkers may prefer to omit. You must reverse the ascent of the south peak in order to regain the bealach between the south peak and the centre peak. Descend from this bealach to regain the corrie and the path back to your starting point.

Climbing the Cobbler's summit block.

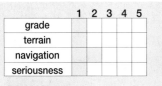

	1	2	3	4	5
grade					
terrain					
navigation					
seriousness					

OS MAP: 56
GR: 360986
DISTANCE: 7 miles (11km)
ASCENT: 1,000m (3,300ft)
TIME: 5 hours

ASSESSMENT: an easy and pleasant round above probably the most beautiful of Scottish lochs.

SEASONAL NOTES: most of the route remains easy under normal snow conditions, but the final section around the rim of the northern corrie and the descent of the north-west ridge require care when iced.

Note for masochists: the Ben Lomond race record (up and down) stands at just over 1 hour.

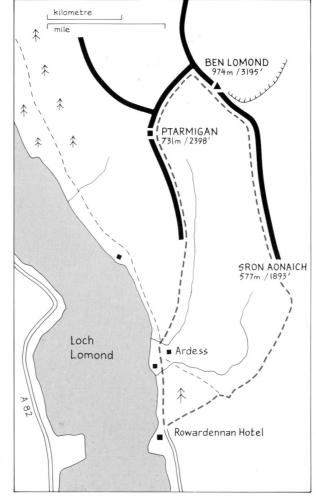

*'What would the world be, once bereft
Of wet and wilderness?
Let them be left.
O let them be left, wildness and wet;
Long live the weeds and the wilderness yet.'*

GERARD MANLEY HOPKINS (Inversnaid)

Ben Lomond, the most southerly Munro in Scotland, stands sentinel over that most beautiful of lochs, Loch Lomond. It is easily accessible from the lowlands and its ascent from the lochside is probably the most popular in the Highlands, apart from Ben Nevis.

An early traveller wrote of the ascent that 'it is very irksome and in some places so steep that we were obliged to crawl on hands and knees'. However, today there is a well-trodden and unmistakable path which will take you all the way to the top. It is advisable to keep to this path to avoid further erosion.

Begin at the car park just beyond the Rowardennan Hotel, at the end of the minor road that runs along the eastern shore of Loch Lomond. The signposted path leaves from behind the toilet block. For the first 200m (650ft) it climbs a clearing in the forest and then it takes to the open hillside for a further 350m (1,150ft) ascent up the shoulder of Sron Aonaich. The convex slopes of Sron Aonaich block the view ahead, but the developing panorama over the island-studded southern reaches of Loch Lomond more than compensates for the effort involved.

The top of Sron Aonaich marks the start of Ben Lomond's plateau-like south ridge, which leads gently to a steep final 200m (650ft) pull up to the summit ridge. The path emerges on the skyline at the lip of a deep, craggy corrie gouged out of the northern side of the mountain. The crags are doubly impressive after the gentle southern aspect of the mountain, but are too vegetatious to provide much rock climbing. The path traverses just below the corrie rim to reach the summit. The summit trig. pillar, perched on the edge of a steep drop to the north, affords an incomparable view of the Arrochar Alps and Southern Highlands.

A return via the subsidiary peak of Ptarmigan completes a fine round. The path drops steeply at first down Ben Lomond's rocky north-west ridge and then bears left to follow Ptarmigan's north ridge. This latter ridge provides lovely walking territory, as the path meanders among rocky knolls and Loch Lomond fills the horizon.

From the final top (Ptarmigan itself) the path descends steeply to follow a broad grassy terrace on the right of the continuing ridge. It eventually reaches the river that tumbles down to Ardess and descends its right bank to reach a dirt track road, which will provide a short lochside stroll back to your starting point.

Ben Lomond is almost constantly under threat from hydro-electric power schemes, farm roads scarring the hillsides and plans to 'improve' amenities for visitors; may it resist these threats and continue to inspire future generations, as it did Gerard Manley Hopkins.

The summit ridge of Ben Lomond.

	1	2	3	4	5
grade					
terrain					
navigation					
seriousness					

OS MAP: 50
GR: 343291
DISTANCE: 11½ miles (18km)
ASCENT: 950m (3,100ft)
TIME: 7½ hours

ASSESSMENT: a classic skyline circuit on one of Scotland's most shapely mountains.

SEASONAL NOTES: the steep bounding ribs of Coire Gaothaich may be impracticable under snow or when iced, but the scenery is magnificent.

• Scottish winter climbing was pioneered in Coire Gaothaich in the 1890s by the newly formed Scottish Mountaineering Club. Central Gully (Grade 1) was first climbed in 1891.

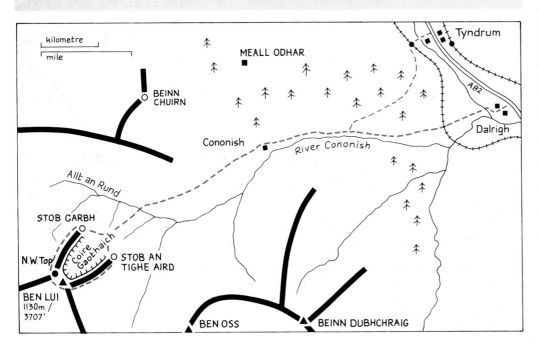

'Light cloud was low, but suddenly, just before we reached Cononish farm, it was blown clear from the Ben, and there soared the mountain, all dazzling white snow and blue shadow, with the azure sky behind, a glorious and unforgettable vision.'

W KERSLEY HOLMES on his favourite mountain (Tramping Scottish Hills, 1946)

Ben Lui is regarded by many as the most beautiful mountain in Scotland. Its twin summits and northern spurs frame the perfect horseshoe of Coire Gaothaich, whose central gully is one of the great classics of Scottish winter mountaineering. Under snow Lui looks truly Alpine, especially when viewed up the glen of the River Cononish from the A82 between Crianlarich and Tyndrum. It is from here that the circuit of the corrie is best approached.

Begin at Dalrigh 1½ mile (2km) east of Tyndrum. Take the Land Rover track on the right, which passes between the houses at Dalrigh, branches right at the next fork and follows the River Cononish for 4 miles (7km). Ben Lui is in view for most of the way and becomes increasingly foreshortened and impressive as you approach it. When the track ends a good path continues, crossing the Allt an Rund and climbing steep grass slopes beside a tumbling burn into Coire Gaothaich. In the bowl of the corrie in springtime you may have to pick your way across avalanche debris from the huge cornice that forms above the central gully.

Exit the corrie on the left, gaining the skyline beyond Stob an Tighe Aird by climbing steep grass slopes among rock outcrops. The steep spur leading up to the summit soon looms overhead. A cairn at its foot marks the start of a bypass path that goes left into a shallow corrie and provides a route to the summit that avoids all difficulties; in mist and when the ground is wet it is advisable to take this path. The *directissima* route climbs the spur directly, following a path up ever-steepening ground until broken outcrops bar the way. A path avoids the outcrops on the left, but the route is still loose and quite exposed for a while, and in places it is necessary to put hand to rock.

Above the outcrops the spur eases off to provide pleasant walking, with vertiginous views down into Coire Gaothaich. A final steepening again requires handwork before you emerge at the summit cairn. The short summit ridge, slung between the two tops, is a grand place from which to admire both the architecture of the corrie and the extensive view, in which Ben Cruachan is prominent, to the west.

To complete the circuit, walk around the corrie rim to the cairn at the north-west top. A short distance beyond are two further cairns, between which will be found the start of the path that descends the steep broken slopes of the right-hand bounding spur of the corrie.

Care is required on the unstable ground, but it is easier going than the ascent route. At the bealach before Stob Garbh the path bears right to descend into the corrie and complete the round.

Ben Lui from near Cononish.

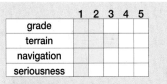

	1	2	3	4	5
grade					
terrain					
navigation					
seriousness					

OS MAP: 51
GR: 457275
DISTANCE: 10 miles (16km)
ASCENT: 1,500m (4,900ft)
TIME: 8 hours

ASSESSMENT: a mainly grassy ridge walk across the two highest and most prominent mountains of the Crianlarich group.

SEASONAL NOTES: care is required on the north-east ridge of Ben More in winter, but otherwise the route is a fine winter expedition with no particular difficulties.

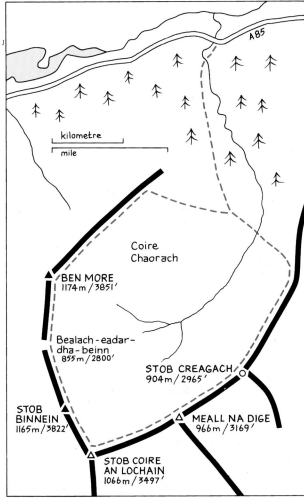

Of all the Ben Mores in Scotland, Crianlarich's Ben More is the highest. With its neighbour Stob Binnein, from which it is separated by a 300m (1,000ft) dip, it is a familiar landmark from both east and west, the unbroken lines of the two mountains' symmetrical cones conveying an impression of great height, especially when dusted with snow. It was a winter ascent here that made Naismith, the 'father' of the Scottish Mountaineering Club, realise that Scottish mountains needed to be treated as seriously as the Alps.

The normal route of ascent is the steep and tedious climb from Benmore Farm, but by far the best route is the circuit of Coire Chaorach, cradled between the eastern arms of Ben More and Stob Binnein. Begin at the car park on the west side of the bridge over the Allt Coire Chaorach, 5 miles (8km) east of Crianlarich on the A85. Just east of the bridge a track leads into the forestry plantations. After about half a mile (1km) keep right at a fork to ford the river, then turn left to follow a quagmire of a path up to the forest edge at GR 458254 – good boots and a sense of humour are essential. Note: at the time of writing the ford can be avoided only by a convoluted and difficult-to-follow route that begins as a path at the back of the car park and after 6-7 minutes turns left to follow clearings marked by yellow tape.

At the forest edge (note this point for later re-entry during the descent), cross the heathery corrie and climb the broad north-

Ben More from near Crianlarich.

east ridge of Stob Creagach. Beyond the summit an undulating descent to a craggy knoll astride a bealach is followed by a steeper ascent to Meall na Dige; after another long, broad bealach the ridge sweeps up elegantly to Stob Coire an Lochain and the castellated summit of Stob Binnein. From Stob Binnein a uniform 300m (1,000ft) descent (a perfect ski run in winter) leads to the Bealach-eadar-dha-beinn, and a stiff re-ascent is required to gain Ben More's rocky summit. It is said that on a clear day you can see half of Scotland from here.

Descend via Ben More's interesting north-east ridge, which is enlivened by one or two outcrops and steepenings, although there is no difficulty. The view before you encompasses the length of Loch Tay, and if it is late in the day the sight of Ben More's monolithic shadow stealing across the moors can be mesmerising. Continue down the ridge until a fence is reached, then follow the fence right into Coire Chaorach to rejoin the ascent route at the forest edge.

	1	2	3	4	5
grade					
terrain					
navigation					
seriousness					

OS MAP: 51
GR: 606382
DISTANCE: 7½ miles (12km)
ASCENT: 820m (2,700ft)
TIME: 5½ hours

ASSESSMENT: an entertaining ridge walk easily reached from a high starting point.

SEASONAL NOTES: one of the most sporting and enjoyable winter routes in the Southern Highlands; unavoidable difficulties are rare, although a measure of competence on snow is required and in hard conditions the wind-swept ridge may become icy.

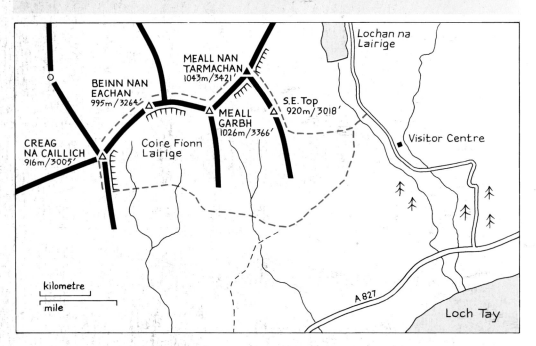

The undulating skyline of the Tarmachan Ridge presents an imposing backdrop to the Falls of Dochart at Killin. For 2 miles (3km) it curves in an 'S' shape above the blue expanse of Loch Tay. At some points it becomes narrow and rocky, and at others broad and grassy. The traverse of its four tops provides a pleasant ramble and scramble that is unfailingly entertaining.

The route begins on the minor road from Loch Tayside to Glen Lyon, which leaves the A827 5 miles (8km) east of Killin. Begin 400m beyond the Ben Lawers Visitor Centre, taking the access track that heads west across the moor to a disused quarry high up in Coire Fionn Lairige. When the track veers left around the south-east shoulder of Meall nan Tarmachan, leave it and climb directly onto the grassy shoulder, which becomes increasingly well-defined as height is gained. At the south-east top the ground falls away to a shallow bealach, and beyond that a steep 130m (400ft) climb leads up through broken craggy ground to the summit.

From the summit the main ridge beckons westwards to the more interesting lower tops. It is broad and knobbly at first and dotted with small knolls and lochans, but soon rears up more steeply to the sharp knob of rock that forms the castellated summit of Meall Garbh. The next section of ridge is the airiest of the day; a short rock step (of no difficulty) leads down to a narrow arête, which projects westwards for some 50m before broadening and dropping down to the narrow defile of the Bealach Riadhailt. Beyond the bealach the best line is obscured by complex terrain, but the skyline is soon regained and the ridge curves upwards around Coire Fionn Lairige to the summit of Beinn nan Eachan.

On the shoulder of Beinn nan Eachan a small cairn commemorates the former status of that point as a Top in Munro's Tables; it is an unremarkable spot and was deleted from the Tables in 1981.

Beyond Beinn nan Eachan the ridge to Creag na Caillich, the fourth and final peak of the day, opens out into a broad, easy walk across a long bealach that provides a pleasant finish to the traverse. The Caillich has three tops that lie at a right-angle to the main ridge and, as you wander out to the end, the other peaks of the Tarmachan Ridge come into fine perspective across Coire Fionn Lairige. From the Caillich a descent can be made to the quarry and back along the access track to your starting point, the only difficulty being a steep craggy section near the top, which is easily bypassed on the west.

On the Tarmachan Ridge west of Meall Garbh.

	1	2	3	4	5
grade					
terrain					
navigation					
seriousness					

OS MAP: 51
GR: 681399
DISTANCE: 10 miles (16km)
ASCENT: 1,350m (4,450ft)
TIME: 7 hours

ASSESSMENT: a circuit of constant interest around a beautiful hidden lochan on the highest mountain in the Southern Highlands.

SEASONAL NOTES: an entertaining but considerable winter challenge. The steep slopes of An Stuc can be treacherous in winter conditions and the inexperienced should stick to the trade route that begins at the Visitor Centre.

The north side of Loch Tay is dominated by massive Ben Lawers, whose height was estimated by early map-makers to exceed 4,000ft (1,220m). Not until 1852 was it demoted to less than that magic figure, which so outraged one local that in 1878 he had it topped up again with a 6m (20ft) summit cairn, which has long since collapsed.

The complete traverse of the 7 Munros of the Lawers group is a considerable undertaking, but is perhaps the best long high-level walk in the Southern Highlands, involving 1,200m (4,000ft) of ascent between first peak and last on the twisting 7 mile (11km) main ridge. Most walkers understandably settle for the well-worn path to the summit that begins at the Ben Lawers Visitor Centre (see Route 5). A more interesting route starts from Lochtayside and takes in the narrowest section of the main ridge around the skyline above Lochan nan Cat, a beautiful, secluded mountain lochan that from the ridge looks like a sitting cat.

Begin at the road to Machuim Farm, at the bridge over the Lawers Burn just outside Lawers village on the A827. Take the track on the right of the horn carver's cottage and, when it turns sharp right, go straight on, keeping to the left of farm buildings. Soon you join a lovely old path that leads past the remains of innumerable stone buildings on the banks of the curiously deep-cutting stream. At one time there were about a dozen mills on the Lawers Burn in the days when Lawers village was a centre of the flax spinning industry.

The path crosses the river (bridge) and becomes indistinct. To find its continuation, climb left onto the high embankment 100m after crossing the bridge. The path joins a track and ends at a small dam at the foot of Meall Garbh. From here, tramp across the moor and climb steep grass slopes to gain the skyline on the right of the summit, then turn left along the ridge to gain the summit itself. A spur ridge on the left makes the summit a difficult spot to locate in mist; if you are in any doubt, keep to the right at the fork in the path. The next Munro on the route (new in 1997) is the imposing prow of An Stuc. The path descends to a gap and winds steeply up the face left of centre. Towards the summit there is a short stretch of easy scrambling (awkward when greasy) that gives the route its Grade 3 rating. An easier bypass path goes right from the gap, but it can be blocked by snow until early summer.

After another steep descent from the summit of An Stuc, a final 300m (1,000ft) climb over Creag an Fhithich (with vertiginous views down to Lochan nan Cat) leads to the summit of Lawers itself. To complete the circuit of the lochan, curve left down Lawers' pleasantly sharp east ridge, which descends to a broad shoulder and then to the stream below the lochan. From here an indistinct path leads back to the dam to rejoin the approach route.

Ben Lawers is a considerable attraction, not only for walkers but also for skiers and botanists. Coire Odhar was the first popular skiing area in Scotland and true mountain skiers still venture here today, far from the mechanised crowds. The traverse of the main ridge under snow is considered to be one of the finest ski-mountaineering expeditions in Scotland. Botanists are attracted by the Alpine flora, prompting the National Trust for Scotland to buy the mountain in 1950, and so easing access for walkers.

Ben Lawers from across Loch Tay.

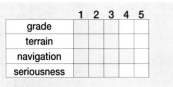

	1	2	3	4	5
grade					
terrain					
navigation					
seriousness					

OS MAP: 50
GR: 078268
DISTANCE: 8 miles (13km)
ASCENT: 1,420m (4,650ft)
TIME: 7 hours

ASSESSMENT: a narrow horseshoe ridge walk that is one of the classic skyline traverses of the Central Highlands.

SEASONAL NOTES: in winter the route is a magnificent expedition for those competent on narrow snow arêtes and iced rock.

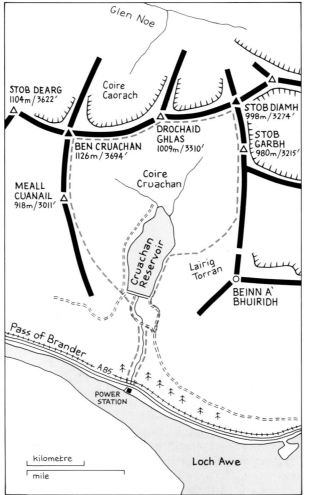

Ben Cruachan is an impressive and beautiful mountain range in miniature, whose seven attractive peaks and narrow supporting ridges rise in splendid isolation between Loch Etive and Loch Awe. The classic Cruachan traverse follows the horseshoe skyline around Coire Cruachan, which holds Cruachan Reservoir.

Begin near Cruachan power station on the A85 by Lochaweside. Paths go up both sides of the Allt Cruachan to the reservoir. The west bank path begins as a dirt road opposite the power station, while the east bank path begins 200m further east and goes under the railway line. The west bank path is better on descent as it affords lovely views over Loch Awe. On descent, note that when approaching the road it branches right at a large boulder 20m before a group of pylons.

The paths climb steeply through woods for 300m (1,000ft) before easing off to reach the Cruachan dam access road. A higher road leads to the right-hand corner of the dam and then a path continues along the shore to the stream that comes down from the Lairig Torran. Once across the stream, make a rising traverse to the ridge leading up to the summit of Stob Garbh. Although the path disappears, it re-establishes itself on the ridge and continues all the way around the skyline.

The going is extremely pleasant on boulder-strewn turf as the ridge leads over Stob Garbh and across a gap to hidden Stob Diamh. Here, the main ridge swings westwards and narrows around the rim of a craggy (unnamed) northern

corrie to climb steeply up the rocky summit slopes of Drochaid Ghlas (optional scrambling). The summit of Drochaid Ghlas lies 50m out along its north ridge, whose rocky crest drops out of sight in a series of steps that provide scenic and easy scrambling above Loch Etive.

Broader slopes continue westwards around the rim of craggy Coire Caorach, but then the ridge narrows again for the final ascent to the fine pointed summit of Ben Cruachan itself. This section is enlivened by a 'granny stopper', an easy scramble down slabs that can be avoided only by a long descent to the left. The crest of the ridge from here to the summit is the narrowest of the day and provides easy scrambling opportunities, while a path lower down avoids all difficulties.

After savouring the immense summit view,

Ben Cruachan from the head of Loch Etive.

descend Cruachan's steep, shattered southern slopes to the bealach before Meall Cuanail. It is possible to descend from here to pick up a track along the west shore of the reservoir, but it is better to continue over Meall Cuanail and descend the gentle grassy slopes to the dam. This will prolong the view over Loch Awe.

	1	2	3	4	5
grade					
terrain					
navigation					
seriousness					

OS MAP: 41
GR: 175566
DISTANCE: 6 miles (10km)
ASCENT: 1,150m (3,750ft)
TIME: 6 hours

ASSESSMENT: a varied route along the glens and ridges of a complex and beautiful mountain.

SEASONAL NOTES: winter difficulties should not be underestimated; the ridges may be corniced and the headwall of Coire Gabhail becomes a steep snow climb.

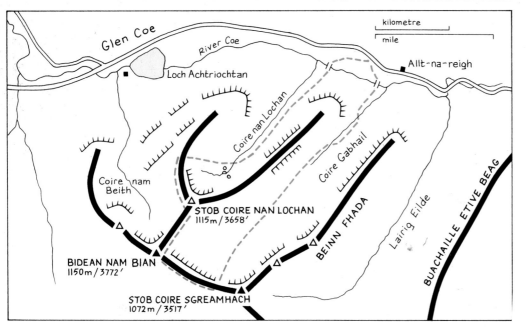

The graceful summit of Bidean nam Bian, the highest mountain in Argyll, lies hidden at the hub of more than 12 miles (20km) of ridges, mostly over 914m (3,000ft). To the north it thrusts out three spurs that terminate in the bold buttresses known as the Three Sisters of Glen Coe, which dramatically shut in that solemn glen on its south side. The glens between the Sisters are of exceptional interest, and Bidean is arguably one of the few mountains that is best approached by its valleys rather than its ridges.

Begin at one of the car parks around the corner from Allt-na-reigh cottage. Paths lead down to a bridge over the River Coe and then a good path continues up the rocky gorge between the first and second Sister. Entertaining scrambling can be had by forsaking the path when it crosses the stream and tackling direct a chaotic boulder-field where the stream disappears.

At 370m (1,200ft) you emerge into flat-bottomed Coire Gabhail (also known as the Lost Valley), a fascinating mountain sanctuary where the MacDonalds used to secrete their cattle (and anyone else's) in times of trouble. The steep surrounding walls give the corrie the appearance of an Alpine cirque; at the entrance an enormous boulder provides scrambling exercise and up on the right a warren of short caves can provide further amusement.

At the far end of the corrie the path continues upwards along the edge of a sheer-sided gorge, and then cairns mark a route up the steep, stony corrie headwall. Once onto the skyline you may wish to detour left (eastwards) to the summit of Stob Coire Sgreamhach, a new Munro in 1997. Heading westwards along the skyline, there is still some distance to go to the summit of Bidean nam Bian, but the ridge is not without interest, especially at one narrow, level section. In misty weather, note that a number of dips are crossed before reaching the true summit, perched at the apex of three ridges.

From the summit, descend the right-hand (north-east) ridge, cross a bealach and re-ascend to Stob Coire nan Lochan. On the descent take care not to be led out left onto the top of vertiginous buttresses, from where there is definitely no way on.

Stob Coire nan Lochan is another fine summit, where the ridge forks to cradle the corrie after which it is named. The left-hand (north-west) ridge gives the more pleasant descent, as it rims the edge of deep gullies which make dramatic winter climbs. Keep going until you reach a broad saddle beyond the cliffs, then cut back right down the gentle slopes to the group of lochans in the corrie. From here a path on the right of the stream descends between the second and third Sisters to reach another bridge over the River Coe, returning you to your starting point.

Stob Coire nan Lochan from the old Glen Coe road.

	1	2	3	4	5
grade					
terrain					
navigation					
seriousness					

OS MAP: 41
GR: 221563
DISTANCE: 8½ miles (14km)
ASCENT: 1,080m (3,550ft)
TIME: 6½ hours

ASSESSMENT: a steep ascent amidst magnificent rock scenery, followed by a pleasant walk along an undulating ridge.

SEASONAL NOTES: an impressive mountain in winter; although the ridge contains no difficulties, the headwall of Coire na Tulaich becomes a steep snow climb, sometimes corniced at the exit.

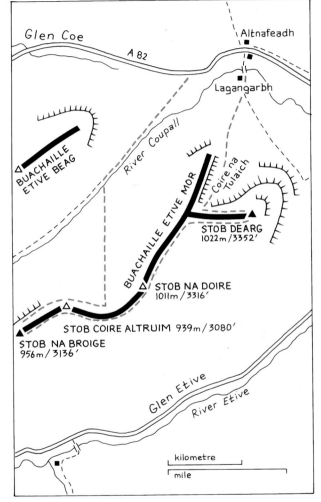

Buachaille Etive Mor is one of the finest mountains in Scotland. On the approach to Glen Coe from the east it rears up, improbably, above the flat expanse of Rannoch Moor like a huge arrow-head, bristling with rock and ice routes. Behind the summit, two further tops and a Munro (new in 1997) punctuate a long backbone, stretching above Glen Etive, and offering a fine but often neglected ridge walk.

For capable scramblers, Curved Ridge (the left edge of the gully to the left of the obvious Crowberry Tower near the summit) is a magnificent ascent route, slightly harder than Aonach Eagach and graded a Moderate rock climb. For walkers, however, the only feasible approach to the Buachaille is the climber's descent route via Coire na Tulaich.

Begin at Altnafeadh, on the Glen Coe road, and take the path over the River Coupall (bridge) past Lagangarbh climbers' hut. The well-worn peaty path crosses the moor and scrambles up the right-hand wall of the gorge of the burn coming down from Coire na Tulaich, which disappears underground in places. (*NB*: the path to the foot of Curved Ridge branches left beneath the cliffs.) Go straight up the scree gully at the head of the corrie (care required), then turn left and climb the summit rockpile of Stob Dearg for the stupendous view over Rannoch Moor. A worthwhile diversion is a short descent over the top to view Crowberry Tower, whose ascent provides an exciting short scramble that is not as hard as it looks and gives a taste of north face

exposure. Imagine Crowberry Ridge below the tower as it is in winter, 'a sensational arête arrayed in shark's fins of translucent ice', as W H Murray described it on the first ascent.

From Stob Dearg, return to the head of Coire na Tulaich (great care is required in mist) and follow the ridge, now grassy and with pools nestling in hollows, as it curves round to the foot of Stob na Doire. A steep, stony traverse of this peak leads to a narrow grassy bealach from where the final two peaks of Stob Coire Altruim and Stob na Broige are soon reached.

The stroll along the final section of ridge, which is level and narrow, provides a pleasant finish to the traverse, and ends on the tranquil dome of Stob na Broige for a very fine view of Loch Etive, far from the busy summit of Stob Dearg. From Stob na Broige, return to the

Buachaille Etive Mor from Rannoch Moor.

grassy bealach at the foot of Stob na Doire and descend the grass slopes to the Lairig Gartain path, which leads back, through the broad trench between Buachaille Etive Mor and Buachaille Etive Beag, to the roadside not far from Altnafeadh.

	1	2	3	4	5
grade					
terrain					
navigation					
seriousness					

ASSESSMENT: the most sensational scramble on the Scottish mainland.

SEASONAL NOTES: this route provides a major winter mountaineering expedition.

OS MAP: 41
GR: 174566
DISTANCE: 6 miles (10km)
ASCENT: 1,000m (3,300ft)
TIME: 7½ hours

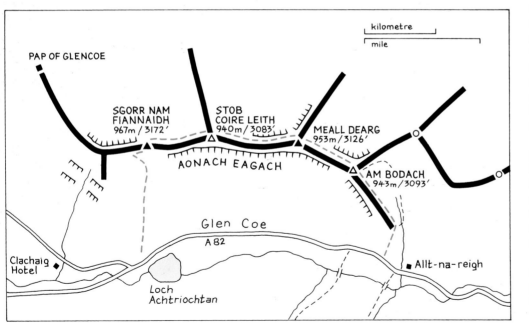

'On a certain day of snow and ice and sunshine I stayed at home while two friends made their first traverse of the ridge. Afterwards one of them told me he was disappointed because it was not as difficult as he had expected. He ought to have been almighty thankful.'

BEN HUMBLE (*On Scottish Hills, 1946*)

Aonach Eagach lays claim to being the finest ridge on the Scottish mainland. For almost 2 miles (3km) its pinnacled crest lines the northern side of Glen Coe, providing exciting – sometimes daunting – scrambling in exposed situations. Those with a good head for heights, who take it slow and easy and savour its situations to the full, will find it an immensely satisfying route. Note that, unlike most scrambles in this book, there is no way of bypassing the awkward sections and, unfortunately, no easy way off down to the glen.

Begin the route at one of the car parks around the corner from Allt-na-reigh cottage, from where paths lead up to the summit of Am Bodach at the east end of the ridge. The easiest route to the summit follows a path into the ravine on the far side of Am Bodach's south-east ridge. This climbs to the skyline at the saddle north-east of Am Bodach.

A more interesting route ascends the south-east ridge directly, where easy scrambling will prepare both mind and body for the excitements to come.

Heading west along the main ridge from the

summit of Am Bodach, the first obstacle is encountered almost immediately in the form of an awkward descent caused by the polished rock. Also, if wearing a rucksack, parts of this section of the route are best tackled by facing inwards.

From the foot of the descent the ridge continues sharply, but more easily, to Meall Dearg, which has a unique place in Scottish mountaineering history: in 1901 it became the final Munro on the list of A E Robertson, the first person to complete all the Munros.

Beyond Meall Dearg, pinnacles bar the way to Stob Coire Leith. There is no way around them, and although the route has been well-worn by generations of climbers, there are several places that will cause you to pause for inspiration and curse the author whose guidebook recommended this route. The last two pinnacles especially involve particularly spectacular scrambling before you can catch your breath on the easy walk to Stob Coire Leith. From here the now easy ridge continues to Sgor nam Fiannaidh, a wonderful viewpoint overlooking Loch Leven.

Unfortunately, there are no pleasant ways back down to the glen from the summit of Sgor nam Fiannaidh. Unless continuing to the Pap of Glencoe, the safest way is to continue westwards along the ridge for a short distance, then descend south-eastwards into a small corrie and continue down steep, rough quartzite slopes to reach the roadside near Loch Achtriochtan. The day ends with a 2½ mile (4km) walk back up the glen to Allt-na-reigh. *NB*: a direct descent to Clachaig Inn, using the steep, loose path beside Clachaig Gully, is not recommended.

Looking east along Aonach Eagach.

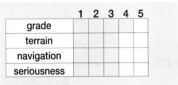

	1	2	3	4	5
grade					
terrain					
navigation					
seriousness					

OS MAP: 41
GR: 168691
DISTANCE: 8½ miles (14km)
ASCENT: 1,500m (4,900ft)
TIME: 7½ hours

ASSESSMENT: a ramble and scramble of unfailing interest along the narrowest ridges of the Mamores, with several airy sections and a magnificent approach walk.

SEASONAL NOTES: a classic but long winter traverse, not suitable for beginners.
The An Garbhanach-An Gearanach ridge and the Devil's Ridge should not be undertaken by those unused to winter ridge walking.

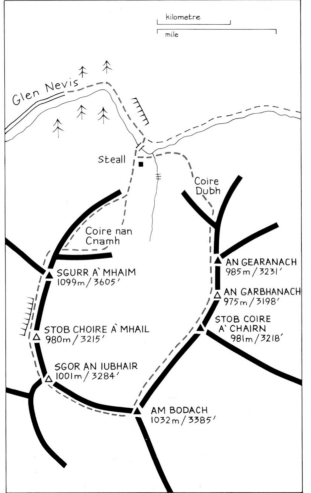

The shapely Mamore range south of Glen Nevis contains over a dozen summits connected by entertainingly narrow ridges. The horseshoe of peaks around Coire a' Mhail above Steall Waterfall provides the best round in the Mamores, with seven tops over 914m (3,000ft). The approach to Steall is, moreover, the most impressive of any mountain route in Scotland.

The route begins at the car park at the end of the Glen Nevis road where the mountains close in on the glen. Ahead lies the unique Nevis gorge, where the Water of Nevis thunders loudly and dramatically over a tangle of enormous boulders.

A path penetrates the gorge high above the river, and clings to the thickly-wooded precipice. Care is needed in places. It debouches into a hidden mountain sanctuary, an enclosed grassy plain at the end of which plunges the 100m (300ft) Steall Waterfall. Keep to the path until the Steall climbers' hut can be seen across the river on the right, then cross the wire bridge to reach it. For many walkers this is the most heart-stopping moment of the day, for the bridge consists of only three wires – one for the feet and one on each side for the hands. The crossing of this swaying tightrope above the turbulent river is not to be recommended for the fainthearted.

Beyond the hut, thread a way up the steep, craggy slopes on the right to gain the north-east ridge of Sgurr a' Mhaim. This leads to the summit without difficulty, but a more

interesting scramble can be had by crossing Coire nan Cnamh on the left and ascending the east ridge, complete with its 'bad step' (an exposed stride).

Continuing south over the summit, the Devil's Ridge is encountered; this begins with an easy descent to a saddle, then a scramble up a slab leads to an airy crest that continues to Stob Choire a' Mhail. The ridge then broadens across a dip to join the main spine of the Mamores at Sgor an Iubhair. Easy grass slopes are now followed eastwards over Am Bodach

to Stob Coire a' Chairn, where the main ridge is left once more for a side ridge that strikes north to complete the horseshoe of Choire a' Mhail. A sharp descent and re-ascent, with optional scrambling, leads to the rocky top of An Garbhanach. Here the ridge narrows briefly to an exposed arête before broadening to the last top of the day, An Gearanach. From here descend easy slopes onto the north-east spur, picking up a good path that zigzags down Coire Dubh and around the foot of Steall Waterfall, to rejoin the path back through the Nevis gorge.

On the summit ridge of An Garbhanach.

The Nevis gorge is given a Himalayan character by its combination of crags, mixed woodland and turbulent waters. It is unique in this country and internationally renowned. The (unsuccessful) 1961 hydro-electric scheme to dam the head of the gorge would have been an act of irredeemable vandalism, and shows the need for adequate countryside protection measures, such as those campaigned for by the Scottish Wild Land Group and the John Muir Trust.

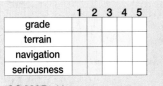

	1	2	3	4	5
grade					
terrain					
navigation					
seriousness					

OS MAP: 41
GR: 186630
DISTANCE: 9 miles (15km)
ASCENT: 1,180m (3,850ft)
TIME: 6½ hours

ASSESSMENT: excellent stalkers' paths ease the ascent to and descent from a typically fine Mamore ridge walk, but the negotiation of Na Gruagaichean's rough north-west top raises the terrain category from 1 to 4. This can be avoided by a descent of the easy south ridge.

SEASONAL NOTES: an excellent winter ridge walk, normally without any major problems except for the negotiation of Na Gruagaichean's north-west top.

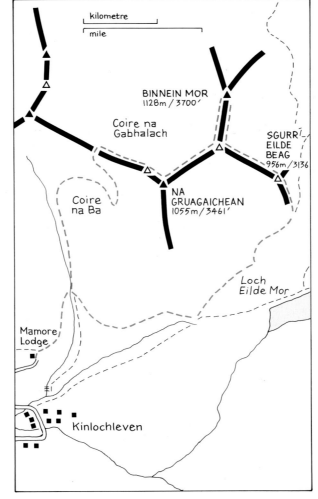

The eastern peaks of the Mamores are best approached from Kinlochleven, from where some excellent stalkers' paths provide easy access to the fine ridge connecting the twin peaks of Na Gruagaichean to the tapering summit crest of Binnein Mor.

The route begins at Mamore Lodge, reached by a short access road that leaves the B863 just east of Kinlochleven (there is a small fee for using the car park). At the T-junction just behind the lodge, go right on a Land Rover track that heads east across the hillside, giving good views back along Loch Leven. At the last right-hand bend before the high point of the track (cairn), branch left on a stalkers' path that crosses the moor and climbs high across the south-east shoulder of Sgurr Eilde Beag to a plateau between Sgurr Eilde Beag and Sgurr Eilde Mor. Just before the high point of the path (cairn), branch left on another excellent path that zigzags up to the cliff-edge perch that is the summit of Sgurr Eilde Beag.

A short stony descent follows and then a broad, grassy shoulder leads up to the south top of Binnein Mor on the main Mamore ridge. Turn right to walk out along the narrowing ridge to Binnein Mor's main summit, which lies at the near end of a sharp, level crest that from many angles gives the mountain the appearance of a ridge-tent. This is the crowning point of the entire Mamore range.

Returning to the south top, follow the main ridge as it sweeps round Coire na Gabhalach, becoming pleasantly narrow in places as it rises

to the summit of Na Gruagaichean. Beyond this point the character of the route changes completely as a deep rocky gap, requiring a steep descent and re-ascent of 60m (200ft), bars the continuation to the nearby north-west top.

The descent is stony, loose and awkward near the foot. The ascent of the far side is an easier route and begins with a short, pleasant scramble (which may be bypassed by a path).

Once over the north-west top, the descent to the bealach at the head of Coire na Ba is also steep, stony and loose. This whole section of the route can be avoided, if necessary, by the easy south ridge that descends from Na Graugaichean's main summit to the Land Rover track.

From the wide bealach at the head of Coire na Ba, a stalkers' path takes a rather convolut-

Binnein Mor from across upper Glen Nevis.

ed route down the steep corrie headwall. It traverses left across the hillside to a junction, cuts back right to another junction at a stream, then descends left, high above the main river; both junctions are cairned. The path eventually rejoins the Land Rover track not far from Mamore Lodge.

	1	2	3	4	5
grade					
terrain					
navigation					
seriousness					

OS MAP: 41
GR: 128718
DISTANCE: 9½ miles (15km)
ASCENT: 1,660m (5,450ft)
TIME: 8½ hours

ASSESSMENT: a classic ridge walk amidst spectacular rock scenery on Britain's highest mountain.

SEASONAL NOTES: a spectacular winter route requiring technical competence on narrow snow ridges and iced rocks; the CMD arête can become a knife-edge of snow and the steep summit slopes of the Ben are dangerous when iced. Even the tourist path is difficult when obliterated by snow.

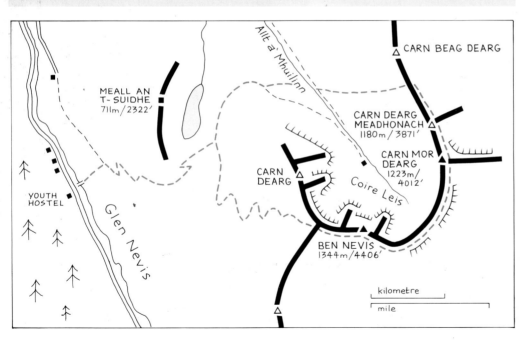

Ben Nevis, monarch of the British hills, is a mountain on the grand scale. Its summit lies only a few hundred feet below the permanent snow line and is in cloud for an average of 300 days per year. To the south and west, its enormous bulk towers over the narrow confines of Glen Nevis, while to the north-east it rims Coire Leis with a 1 mile (1½ km) face of 600m (2,000ft) cliffs.

The normal route of ascent for baggers is the tiresome 'tourist' path up the western slopes, but the Ben deserves better. The true mountain lover will forsake the normal route for the skyline of Coire Leis, a classic ridge walk with some spectacular situations.

Begin at the youth hostel in Glen Nevis and take the engineered tourist path up the badly eroded hillside, joining the old track from Achintee Farm that climbs steadily onto the plateau between Meall an t-Suidhe and Carn Dearg. At a sharp right fork alongside Lochan Meall an t-Suidhe, take the path that continues straight on towards the Allt a' Mhuilinn. When the path descends right towards Coire Leis, leave it and pick a route across the Allt a' Mhuilinn and up the steep, grass slopes of Carn Dearg Meadhonach. The ascent is relentless, but the views into Coire Leis and westwards over Loch Eil more than compensate. From the summit a short scramble to the first top on the pinnacled east ridge makes a pleasant diversion.

From Carn Dearg Meadhonach, continue across a short dip to the summit of Carn Mor Dearg, beyond which the ridge narrows to form the famous 'CMD arête' – the rocky crest that rims the head of Coire Leis. Those with a head for heights will revel in boulder-hopping along the crest, while a well-worn path among the boulders provides easier going for the less balletic. All the while the spectacular north face of the Ben is close at hand, giving the route a real mountaineering flavour. Beyond a small top, the arête veers right and provides easier walking until it abuts against the south-east slopes of the Ben, where enjoyable scrambling will be found at the cliff edge above Coire Leis. A final stiff 300m (1,000ft) climb up stony slopes is required to reach the roof of Britain. The view is considerable, and there is much of interest on the summit plateau, including the forlorn ruins of the old Observatory.

Descend via the tourist path, taking great navigational care across the plateau in adverse weather. As you descend the seemingly interminable zigzags, you will at last thank the author of the guidebook who suggested that you avoid their ascent.

Important note: Under snow the descent from the summit plateau is dangerous and requires accurate navigation, especially in cloud. In February 1994 people were killed here on three separate occasions. From the summit trig. point, walk 150m on a grid bearing of 231° (236° magnetic in 1994), then follow a grid bearing of 281° (286° magnetic in 1994) to clear the plateau in the direction of the tourist path.

Approaching the CMD Arête.

	1	2	3	4	5
grade					
terrain					
navigation					
seriousness					

OS MAP: 41
GR: 252807
DISTANCE: 17½ miles (28km)
ASCENT: 1,620m (5,300ft)
TIME: 10½ hours

ASSESSMENT: one of the longest and most entertaining ridge walks on the mainland.

SEASONAL NOTES: in winter, sections of the ridge narrow to snow arêtes, which provide a classic traverse for competent winter walkers. If time is short, the route can be curtailed by a descent northwards from Stob Coire Easain over Beinn na Socaich.

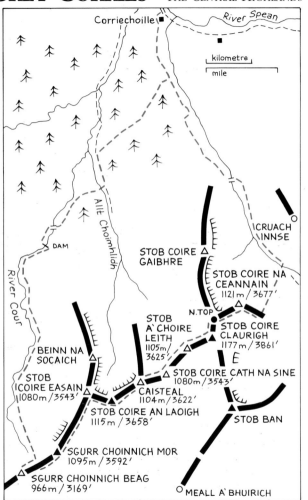

The peaks east of Ben Nevis and the Aonachs are less massive and more graceful, forming a group of a dozen tops that are linked by a high, sometimes sharp, ridge. They are collectively known as the Grey Corries, after the colour of their quartzite summits. Their traverse makes a magnificent ridge walk, rivalling that of the Mamores to the south. The best approach is from the north, where subsidiary ridges jut out between deep corries that hold snow late into the year.

Begin at Corriechoille Farm at the end of the minor road from Spean Bridge, and go along the beautifully wooded south bank of the River Spean. Take the Land Rover track south, past the farm and past a right fork, and continue straight on over the Lochaber Narrow Gauge Railway line, along the old drove road through the forest to the Lairig Leacach. Leave the track just before the foot of the craggy north-east spur of Stob Coire na Ceannain and scramble up beside a burn on the right to reach a shallow corrie. Bear right, up stony slopes, then left along a more well-defined ridge, to reach the summit.

The ridge proper now begins with the best scramble of the day along the narrow connecting ridge to Stob Choire Claurigh, the highest of the Grey Corries. The scrambling is easy going and and can avoided, if necessary. From the summit the tortuous twistings of the Grey Corries ridge are spread out before you, with Ben Nevis providing a soaring backdrop. The narrow ridge twists and turns and undulates

over a succession of tops, never dipping below 1,020m (3,350ft), and providing a glorious stravaig of such interest that the ascents seem almost effortless.

At Stob Coire Easain the ridge does a 90° turn left, narrows to a deeply-fissured quartzite pavement and descends to a 940m (3,100ft) bealach, before rising once more to the shapely summit of Sgurr Choinnich Mor. Beyond lies the last top on the ridge, the grassy hump of Sgurr Choinnich Beag; though hardly a 'grey corrie' there is no excuse for not climbing it.

Returning to the bealach between Sgurr Choinnich Mor and Sgurr Choinnich Beag, descend into the remote upper valley of the River Cour and follow the right bank of the river down beside inviting pools and cascades. Lower down, a forest road eases the going for

The Grey Corries ridge from Sgurr Choinnich Mor.

the last 4 miles (7km) back to Corriechoille. It begins on the left bank of the river at a dam; turn left at a T-junction after crossing the Allt Choimhlidh, then keep right at a fork to emerge from the trees and rejoin the outward track above Corriechoille.

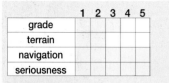

	1	2	3	4	5
grade					
terrain					
navigation					
seriousness					

OS MAP: 42
GR: 615835
DISTANCE: 22½ miles (36km)
ASCENT: 930m (3,050ft)
TIME: 11 hours

Boathouse approach (each way):
5½ miles (9km), **out** 150m (500ft)
back 50m (150ft), 2 hours
Ascent from Boathouse:
11½ miles (18km), 730m (2,400ft),
7 hours

ASSESSMENT: two superb ridges
provide very easy scrambling with a
real mountaineering flavour on an
exceptional mountain.

SEASONAL NOTES: both the Long
and Short Leachas are considerable
undertakings under snow, and the
summit plateau of Ben Alder is best
avoided in foul weather. In case of
difficulty, the easiest descent route
from the summit is to go west for
1 mile (1½km), then north to reach
the Bealach Dubh at GR 481732.

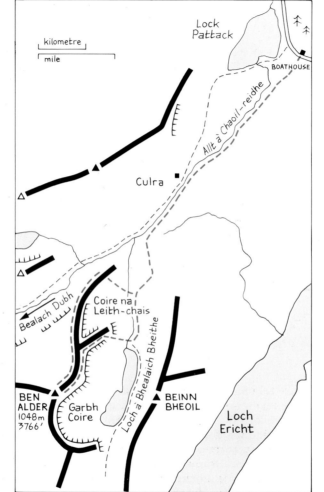

Massive, majestic and remote Ben Alder is a
mountain which attracts the devotion of
all those who love the wild places of Scotland
and, as further enticement, its two narrow
north-east ridges, the Long Leachas and the
Short Leachas, provide an exciting circuit for
the mountain walker. The long approach route
along the Land Rover track from Dalwhinnie
makes any route on the mountain a very long
day; many people cycle in, camp or stay
overnight at Culra bothy.

The track begins just south of Dalwhinnie
railway station and crosses the line; cars can be
driven to a locked gate 1½ miles (2km) along.
Follow the track along Loch Erichtside as far as
Ben Alder Lodge, then branch right to reach a
shed (the Boathouse) near Loch Pattack. From
the Boathouse an excellent stalkers' path crosses the moor to Ben Alder. Opposite Culra on
the far bank of the Allt a' Chaoil-reidhe (no
bridge), the going deteriorates for a while
where a new stony track negotiates the area
flooded during the storms of 1990, but the good
path soon reappears. It climbs far to the left,
before swinging back right to traverse across
the hillside towards Ben Alder. When it turns
left again along the bank of the stream coming
down from Loch a' Bhealaich Bheithe, cross the
stream and make directly across the bowl of
Coire na Leith-chais in front of you to gain the
right-hand bounding ridge – the Long Leachas.

The ridge rises in a series of humps. There
are two abrupt steepenings, up which a path
finds the line of least resistance, and then the

ridge narrows excitingly, breaking out into pinnacles as it approaches the summit plateau. The path provides plenty of handwork, but it is barely a scramble. Off-path, extremely pleasant scrambling can be sought in superb situations.

Once on the vast summit plateau, almost 400 acres (4 sq km) in extent, turn left and follow the plateau rim over a rise and along the edge of Garbh Coire's impressive cliffs to reach the summit. Note that in misty conditions the summit cairn lies a couple of hundred metres back from the cliff edge.

Retrace your steps along the plateau rim until just beyond the rise to find the start of the Short Leachas. Again, there are some fine situations and plenty of handwork is required, but

On the Long Leachas, Ben Alder.

it barely amounts to a scramble.

To avoid the buttress at the foot of the ridge, descend via the heathery slopes on the right, then cross over the moor to rejoin the approach path at the mouth of Loch a' Bhealaich Bheithe.

	1	2	3	4	5
grade					
terrain					
navigation					
seriousness					

OS MAP: 40
GR: 906808
DISTANCE: 13 miles (21km)
ASCENT: 1,400m (4,600ft)
TIME: 8 hours

ASSESSMENT: an entertaining horseshoe ridge that gains in interest as it progresses.

SEASONAL NOTES: a rewarding winter traverse, but of testing length and one that requires care on its narrow and steep sections.

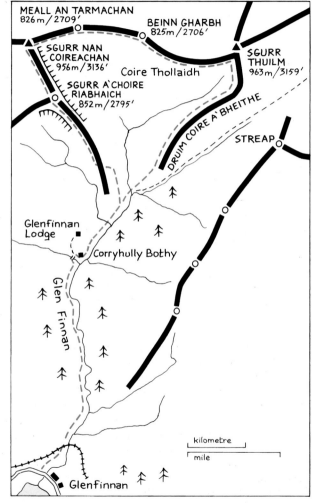

'...as near perfect as anything terrestrial can be.'

W KERSLEY HOLMES' verdict on the route (Tramping Scottish Hills, 1946)

In the district of Locheil, north-west of Fort William, lies a fine group of mountains well-hidden from the A830 Mallaig road but rendered easily accessible by deep glens carrying good tracks. The finest route in the area is the horseshoe circuit of Sgurr Thuilm and Sgurr nan Coireachan above Coire Thollaidh.

Begin on the A830 at Glenfinnan, where Prince Charlie raised his standard at the start of the 1745 Jacobite Rebellion. The area has many associations with Charlie; following his defeat at Culloden, he crossed the Locheil hills no less than three times to escape from his pursuers.

Take the private road to Glenfinnan Lodge that begins on the west side of the bridge over the River Finnan. The road goes under the railway viaduct, built in 1899 and said to contain the remains of a horse and cart that fell into one of the hollow pillars during construction. It continues along the right bank (left side) of the river beside forestry plantations.

After 2½ miles (4km), at the bridge over the Allt a' Chaol-ghlinne, branch right at a T-junction to follow a Land Rover track past Corryhully bothy to the foot of Druim Coire a' Bheithe, the south-west ridge of Sgurr Thuilm which dominates the view ahead. Strike up the ridge on easy grass slopes and continue over a

subsidiary top to reach the main summit. Charlie and his followers waited here all day while redcoats scoured the glens, then escaped northwards under cover of darkness.

The ridge to Sgurr nan Coireachan twists and undulates westwards for 2½ miles (4km). It is mainly broad and grassy, though with some rock outcrops where mild scrambling can be sought. It descends over a subsidiary top to a saddle and then rises over a succession of tops, of which Beinn Gharbh and Meall an Tarma-chan are named on the OS map, to the main summit, providing a pleasant stravaig with ever-widening views westwards over Loch Morar to the glistening sea. Old fence posts mark most of the route.

Sgurr nan Coireachan marks the end of the main ridge, but the most interesting section of the route is still to come: the south-east ridge of Sgurr nan Coireachan, which completes the horseshoe, narrows along the edge of cliffs to the minor summit of Sgurr a' Choire Riabhaich,

Sgurr a' Choire Riabhaich (left) and Sgurr nan Coireachan (right) from Druim Coire a' Bheithe.

then steepens and narrows once more before finally opening out. It makes a fitting finish to a fine round. Near the foot of the ridge, just before the last short rise, descend left to pick up an excellent stalkers' path that leads gently around the nose of the ridge. From here you can rejoin the Land Rover track back to Corryhully bothy and your starting point.

	1	2	3	4	5
grade					
terrain					
navigation					
seriousness					

OS MAP: 33 or 40
GR: 988916
DISTANCE: 14 miles (22km)
ASCENT: 1,180m (3,850ft)
TIME: 9 hours

ASSESSMENT: an adventurous route along a complex rocky ridge leading to a classic West Highland peak.

SEASONAL NOTES: a classic winter traverse, full of entertaining problems – though not a route to be attempted by the inexperienced.

Note that late snow in the gully below the Feadan may cause unexpected difficulties.

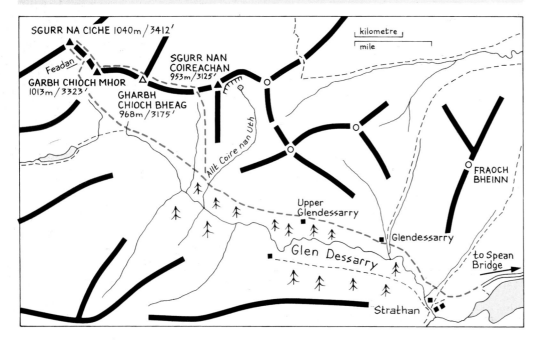

Few peaks in the Highlands excite the imagination as much as Sgurr na Ciche (meaning 'breast-shaped peak'), whose steep symmetrical summit cone soars skywards like a miniature Matterhorn. The route to it and its equally well-named neighbour Garbh Chioch Mhor (meaning 'big, rough, breast-shaped peak') begins at the western end of Loch Arkaig, reached by a long winding road from Spean Bridge. From the road-end take the Land Rover track that continues straight on and bear right at a fork after ten minutes to follow it up Glen Dessarry.

The track passes Glendessarry Farm and ends at Upper Glendessarry Cottage. When you reach the fence around the cottage, go over the stile on the right to pick up the path that continues along the glen above forestry plantations. Follow the path as far as the Allt Coire nan Uth, then take a direct line up the hillside to the Bealach nan Gall below Garbh Chioch Bheag's eastern end.

The terrain now becomes rougher as the skyline is followed westwards over the rugged Garbh Chiochs. An impressive dry stone wall follows the crest of the ridge and a path accompanies it, meandering over and around the many rock outcrops as it climbs over a hump and rises steeply to the summit of Garbh Chioch Bheag. Opportunities for some pleasant scrambling abound.

The ridge continues to undulate as it crosses to the summit of Garbh Chioch Mhor; if you keep to the crest there are some considerable drops into rough Coire nan Gall on the right, but no problems will be encountered. Between Garbh Chioch Mhor and Sgurr na Ciche is the gap known as the Feadan na Ciche, whose name, meaning 'whistle', is best appreciated on a windy day. There are some major crags to be avoided, both on the descent to it and on the re-ascent from it, and from hereon it is best to keep to the path.

The descent begins with a very easy scramble before steepening over rough ground. On re-ascent to Sgurr na Ciche, the path goes far left to avoid crags, then cuts back right up a boulder ruckle to reach the rooftop summit. The superb summit panorama includes a magnificent view across the mountains of the Knoydart peninsula to the small isles and the jagged Cuillin of Skye.

The descent begins with a return to the Feadan. From here, go down the bouldery gully on the south side until below the crags of Garbh Chioch Mhor, where a curious, level grassy terrace, dotted with erratic boulders, will be found leading south-east around the crags. At the end of the terrace cross a spur ridge and descend the pleasant grass slopes beside a small stream to rejoin the path back to Upper Glendessary.

Sgurr na Ciche (centre right) from Loch Quoich.

Route 18: LADHAR BHEINN • THE WESTERN HIGHLANDS

	1	2	3	4	5
grade					
terrain					
navigation					
seriousness					

OS MAP: 33
GR: 949066
DISTANCE: 20 miles (33km)
ASCENT: 1,830m (6,050ft)
TIME: 12 hours

Barrisdale approach (each way): 6 miles (10km), 300m (1,000ft), 3 hours. Ascent from Barrisdale: 8 miles (13km), 1,230m (4,050ft), 6 hours

ASSESSMENT: a route of great stature, whose approach, ascent and views all demand superlatives.

SEASONAL NOTES: the route is best done on a long, hot summer's day. In winter Stob a' Chearcaill's snowy ledges and ice-glazed rock and Stob a' Choire Odhair's narrow crest provide a major test of winter mountaineering skills.

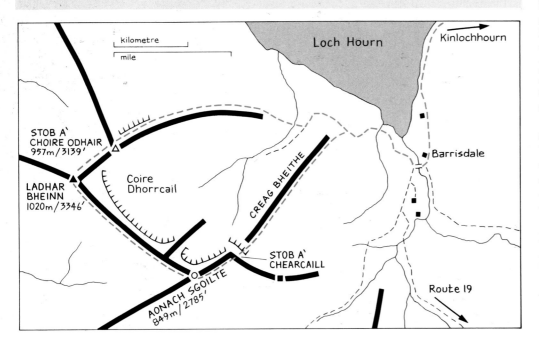

Ladhar Bheinn, the most westerly Munro on the mainland, is regarded by many people (including the author) as the most beautiful mountain in the British Isles. It is a mountain of soaring ridges, spectacular corries, testing remoteness and stunning panoramic views. The wonderful approach route, which provides marvellous views of the mountain's unusual topography, is as for its neighbour Luinne Bheinn and is described in Route 19.

From the bothy at Barrisdale Bay, cross the bridge over the River Barrisdale and take the stalkers' path on the right that crosses the lochside flats and zigzags over the shoulder of Creag Bheithe into Coire Dhorrcail. Leave the path on the shoulder and climb up the rough left bounding ridge of the corrie, which rises in a series of steps to the foot of the enormous shark's fin of rock that is Stob a' Chearcaill.

The route up the Stob climbs a succession of narrow ledges. The scrambling is mostly easy, but there are one or two hard sections and the exposure is considerable; if you are not happy after the first few moves, turn back – all difficulties can be bypassed on steep grass slopes to the left.

Above the Stob a narrow section of ridge leads pleasantly across a small dip to the summit of Aonach Sgoilte, where the main ridge turns sharp right to follow the rim of the rocky headwall of Coire Dhorrcail. After a gradual descent, passing a prominent spur ridge that bisects the corrie, an abrupt steepening, easily negotiated by a good path, leads down to the low point on the corrie rim. On the far side of the dip two short easy scrambles begin the steep re-ascent around the main cliffs; there is much handwork but no real difficulty. Higher up, the going eases off for a while, but there are still two more short dips to cross as the ridge becomes increasingly complex.

On the final steepening to the summit, a step-up onto a large boulder gives small pause for thought, but the pointed top that has been in sight all day is now within reach. The true summit lies less than five minutes further away, the second of three tops on a graceful ridge that curves out towards the western horizon. There are views to die for of the Hebrides and of the mountains crowding the confines of Loch Hourn.

A descent over the sharp subsidiary top of Stob a' Choire Odhair completes the round of Coire Dhorrcail in grand style. The ridge descends steeply from Ladhar Bheinn's first top and narrows (with some exposure) as it crosses the summit of the Stob to descend steeply once more into the grassy confines of the corrie. Once into the corrie, cross the river to pick up the stalkers' path back to Barrisdale.

Ladhar Bheinn from the Loch Hourn path.

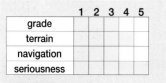

	1	2	3	4	5
grade					
terrain					
navigation					
seriousness					

OS MAP: 33
GR: 949066
DISTANCE: 19 miles (31km)
ASCENT: 1,580m (5,200ft)
TIME: 11 hours

Barrisdale approach (each way): 6 miles (10km), 300m (1,000ft), 3 hours. Ascent from Barrisdale: 7 miles (11km), 980m (3,200ft), 5 hours

ASSESSMENT: an attractive twin-topped mountain characterised by rugged ridges and magnificent coastal views.

SEASONAL NOTES: the route is best done on a long, hot summer's day. In winter the snow-fields that build up on the final section of the north-east ridge above Coire Glas can be treacherous, and the steep upper section of the north-west ridge may also pose problems.

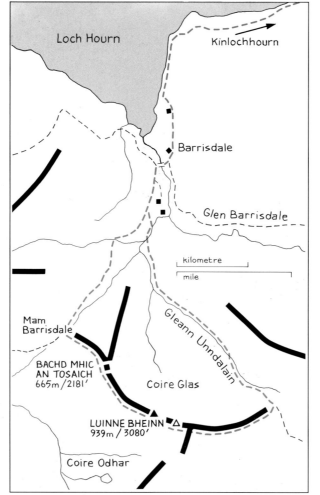

The ascent of Luinne Bheinn has a satisfying symmetry, using two fine stalkers' paths and two interesting ridges to traverse its attractive twin tops. As befitting mountains of the stature of Luinne Bheinn and its neighbour Ladhar Bheinn (Route 18), they are not easy to reach. They stand in one of the most rugged, beautiful and inaccessible parts of the country – the Knoydart peninsula – between the two fjord-like lochs of Loch Hourn and Loch Nevis.

The nearest starting point is Kinlochhourn, at the end of the minor road along Loch Garry from the A87. Park at the farm (small charge).

The 6-mile (9½km) path along the south shore of Loch Hourn to Barrisdale Bay is one of the finest coastal walks in Scotland. Few paths have such wonderful views and such ambience, although you may need to remind yourself of this on the long walk back, when the several short ascents seem much longer. Most walkers backpack into Barrisdale, where there is a campsite and bothy at GR 872042 (often busy, so take a tent just in case).

From the bothy, follow the main track across the River Barrisdale and keep straight on when it bears left to a cottage after 250m. At a fork after a further 250m, take the left branch and follow a lovely path up into the hidden valley of Gleann Unndalain and the bealach at its head. The craggy slopes on the right of the bealach, which mark the start of Luinne Bheinn's north-east ridge, are typical of what is to come – a complex crest bristling with outcrops. There is no difficulty, but the easiest route around the outcrops is not always obvious. The going is rough, but an indistinct path develops and improves as you gain height. Scramblers will find more than enough to keep them happy.

Eventually you reach the junction with a spur that descends towards Meall Buidhe, the third of Knoydart's Munros and one that tigers may wish to append to the route on a long summer's day (add another 3 hours). At the junction the main ridge turns sharp right and ascends more steeply, with handwork required in a couple of places. You emerge on Luinne Bheinn's east top, with the higher west top only a few minutes away across a small intervening dip.

Continuing westwards from the summit around the rim of Coire Glas, a pleasant stroll takes you across one minor top to another, which turns out to be the top of a steep shoulder. A path winds its way down the shoulder among grass and boulders and reaches a complex, knolly plateau named Bachd Mhic an Tosaich. Trend leftwards to reach the Mam Barrisdale and pick up the second stalkers' path of the day, which, although boggy in places, will return you in relentlessly gentle fashion back to Barrisdale.

Luinne Bheinn (centre back) from near the summit of Ladhar Bheinn.

	1	2	3	4	5
grade					
terrain					
navigation					
seriousness					

OS MAP: 33
GR: 843105
DISTANCE: 6 miles (10km)
ASCENT: 1,070m (3,500ft)
TIME: 5 hours

ASSESSMENT: a top-of-the world walk above stunning seascapes.

SEASONAL NOTES: under snow the steepness of Beinn Sgritheall's slopes and the consequences of a slip should not be underestimated; the narrow section may be awkward.

'The view remains in my mind as perhaps the most beautiful I have seen in Scotland.'

SIR HUGH MUNRO

Beinn Sgritheall is a mountain apart. Isolated from the tangle of peaks in the neighbouring districts of Knoydart and Kintail, it rises in one great sweep from the north shore of Loch Hourn, like an enormous tent whose roof consists of a half mile (1km) ridge. The lochside slopes steepen from grass and woods to scree, hardly inviting an ascent in an area of outstanding peaks. Yet this gives a misleading impression of the mountain, for its northern flank has some fine corries and the traverse of the east and west ridges makes a wonderful walk, quite exposed in one section, on a mountain whose summit seems detached from the earth.

Begin at the beautiful village of Arnisdale at the end of the long minor road that leaves the A87 at Shiel Bridge. From the bridge over the river that comes down from the Bealach Arnasdail, go straight up the left bank (right side) behind the row of cottages that front the bay. Open hillside is soon reached, and a path of sorts climbs beside an old fence past some fine waterfalls. There is no respite from the remorseless steepness, but height is gained fast.

Follow the line of the fence where it crosses the river and continues to a lochan in the jaws of the bealach beneath the craggy north-west face of Beinn na h-Eaglaise. From here, climb the steepening cone that forms the east top of

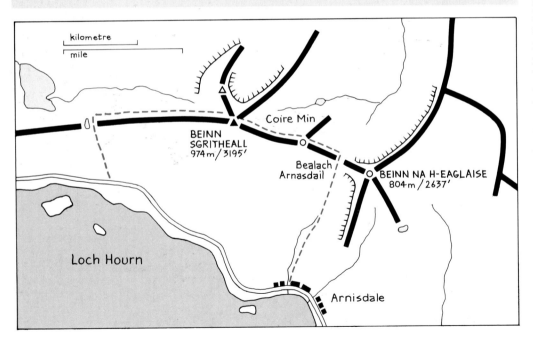

Beinn Sgritheall; with any luck you will find a path to the left of the crest which will ease the ascent of the final stony slopes leading to the flat summit.

The broad grassy ridge that continues round the rim of Coire Min to the main summit provides one of the most pleasant walks to be found on any Scottish mountain. The slopes down to Loch Hourn and the open sea are hidden by their steepness, and the sensation is one of being isolated from the earth. The view of the Knoydart mountains and across the mouth of Loch Hourn to the island of Rum is stunning. Just before the summit the ridge narrows appreciably around the narrow corrie headwall; there is some exposure but there should be no difficulty.

Descend to the foot of the rocky west ridge on a good path, reaching a lochan that completes Beinn Sgritheall's symmetry. Just before

Beinn Sgritheall from across Loch Hourn.

the lochan a cairn on a boulder marks the start of a cairned path that meanders down steep grass and craggy wooded slopes to the roadside. The path is difficult to follow lower down, and the author has yet to discover exactly where it reaches the road. The day ends with a lochside stroll back to Arnisdale.

	1	2	3	4	5
grade					
terrain					
navigation					
seriousness					

OS MAP: 33
GR: 968143
DISTANCE: 7 miles (11km)
ASCENT: 1,040m (3,400ft)
TIME: 6 hours

ASSESSMENT: the most exciting ridge scramble in the Western Highlands, with a path that enables all difficulties to be avoided, if necessary.

SEASONAL NOTES: for experienced winter mountaineers only, especially if the path that avoids the scrambling sections is obliterated by snow.

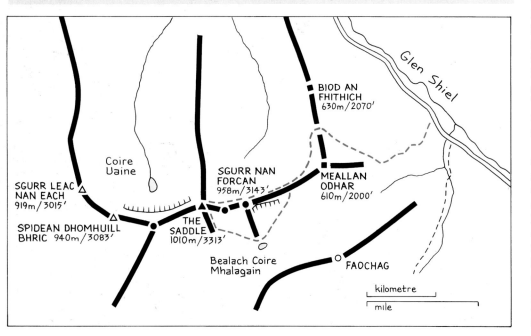

From Loch Cluanie to Loch Duich the deep narrow confines of Glen Shiel carry the A87 north to Kyle of Lochalsh and Skye, and no other glen makes so many fine mountains so easily accessible. With nine Munros to the south of the road and eleven to the north, there is enough here to repay many a visit.

The finest mountain in Glen Shiel is universally acknowledged to be the Saddle – a complex peak of craggy corries and long ridges tapering to graceful twin summits (whose intervening dip forms 'the saddle'). The mountain's long northern ridges make a fine circuit from Shiel Bridge, but for seekers after sensation, the finest ridge of all is the east ridge over Sgurr nan Forcan, and few explore beyond. If taken direct, the Sgurrnan Forcan ridge ranks alongside Aonach Eagach (route 10) and the Torridon ridges as one of the most exciting on the mainland, and it is certainly the classic scramble of the Western Highlands.

Begin in Glen Shiel 300m north of the bridge over the Allt Mhalagain. Look for an excellent stalkers' path that leaves the roadside, meanders up the east ridge of Meallan Odhar and cuts right to the bealach below Biod an Fhithich. From here, a path goes left to the foot of the Forcan ridge and takes a grassy route up the first steep rise, with one or two pieces of handwork to give you a foretaste of what is to come. On breasting the rise, the rocky summit pyramid of Sgurr nan Forcan bursts into view, buttressed by great slabs of rock, and here the excitement really begins.

The arête leading up to the summit is extremely sharp in places and a few sections provide hard scrambling, but the exposure is not great. On closer inspection the route onwards is usually easier than it looks; a summer path below the crest on the right avoids all difficulties if necessary. Beyond the summit of Sgurr nan Forcan the excitement continues: an initial steep descent requires care and further on, towards the east top of the Saddle, a knife edge provides some particularly interesting scrambling; a path again avoids all difficulties.

Beyond the Saddle's main summit, the ridge continues quite narrowly over the west top and around the head of Coire Uaine to Spidean Dhomhuill Bhric and Sgurr Leac nan Each, both of which are worthy objectives if you wish to extend the route. Otherwise, from the main summit, descend a steep grass and boulder slope to the south and bear left towards the Bealach Mhalagain, aiming for two small lochans just above the bealach to the left. The cliffs that form the south side of the Sgurr nan Forcan ridge look very impressive from here. A few metres further down, a path beside a wall contours beneath Sgurr nan Forcan to rejoin the ascent route at the foot of the east ridge.

At the summit of the Saddle above the Sgurr nan Forcan ridge.

	1	2	3	4	5
grade					
terrain					
navigation					
seriousness					

OS MAP: 33
GR: 961211
DISTANCE: 12 miles (19km)
ASCENT: 1,590m (5,200ft)
TIME: 9 hours

ASSESSMENT: the classic West Highland ridge walk.

SEASONAL NOTES: a lengthy but exceptional winter traverse, whose many steep sections may require winter mountaineering skills.

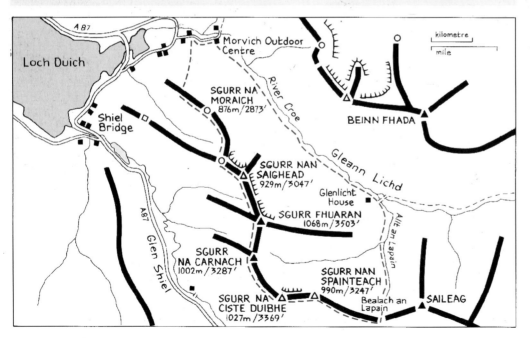

The view of the steep-sided Five Sisters of Kintail from the Glenelg road across Loch Duich is one of the most photographed in the Western Highlands, and the consistently entertaining ridge walk/scramble that connects the summits is justifiably famed.

From the car park at Kintail Countryside Centre in Strath Croe, walk up the road for 500m and take the Land Rover track that branches right along Gleann Lichd to Glenlicht House (a private hut). A path continues beside the River Croe and forks just before a bridge. Keep right to cross the flats at the head of the glen and reach the confluence with the Allt an Lapain. Cross the river here and climb steep grass slopes into the bowl of a small corrie and the Bealach an Lapain on the skyline directly behind.

Now begins the series of steep ascents and descents that will take you over the Five Sisters, beginning with a narrowing ridge that climbs over a succession of rises to the first hard-won summit of the day – Sgurr nan Spainteach, the 'sixth sister' hidden from Loch Duich. From here a rocky descent, requiring handwork, leads to a short rise and then an abrupt drop, negotiated by an easy scramble. A curious hollow on the bealach below may cause confusion in mist. A straightforward ascent brings underfoot Sgurr na Ciste Duibhe (the first Sister) and then gentler slopes lead down to the next bealach before a steep rise to Sgurr na Carnach (the second Sister, a new Munro in 1997). More handwork follows on the descent of a rocky

gully before the ridge eases off to the next bealach and a steep pull brings you to the summit of Sgurr Fhuaran (the third Sister).

The path along the ridge now descends steeply left and then cuts back right (to avoid awkward ground) before easing off across the next bealach and climbing pleasantly along the edge of impressive slabs to the summit pyramid of Sgurr nan Saighead (the fourth Sister). Beyond here the route rims yet more imposing cliffs – great slates of rock sliced so cleanly that they seem unnatural – and then a small rise is crossed and more handwork leads up to the north-west top of Sgurr nan Saighead. Here the ridge splits and the path forks. Keep right on the broader slopes that lead out to Sgurr na

The first three of the Five Sisters from Saileag.

Moraich (the fifth Sister), and then descend very steep grass slopes back to the roadside. To avoid craggy ground, go down the north-west ridge at first then cut back right. If the grass is wet and slippery it may be best to continue all the way down the ridge.

	1	2	3	4	5
grade					
terrain					
navigation					
seriousness					

OS MAP: 33
GR: 054115
DISTANCE: 8 miles (13km)
ASCENT: 1,360m (4,450ft)
TIME: 7 hours

ASSESSMENT: a narrow undulating ridge walk, typical of the Glen Shiel mountains.

SEASONAL NOTES: winter parties may expect to encounter narrow snow arêtes in places.

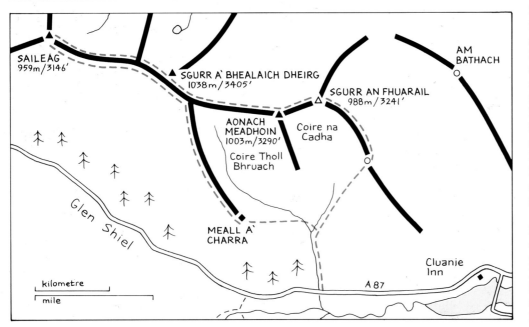

The group of three Munros east of the Five Sisters of Kintail are more retiring than their more famous neighbours; from many roadside viewpoints their summits are hidden behind forestry plantations. Yet they have much in common with the Five Sisters, offering wonderful high-level walking along narrow ridges, with wild corries to the north and plunging grass slopes to the south. Moreover, unlike on the Five Sisters, two subsidiary ridges ease the approach and enable a fine circuit to be made.

Begin at the bridge over the Allt Coire Tholl, Bhruach 1½ miles (2km) west of Cluanie Inn on the A87, and take the path up the left bank (right side) of the river to the foot of Coire na Cadha. From here, climb steep grass slopes to the bump on the skyline that marks the top of the south-east ridge of Sgurr an Fhuarail, then turn left to follow a path along the ridge. The ridge becomes immediately interesting as it narrows invitingly around Coire na Cadha. It crosses a dip and narrows over the summit of Sgurr an Fhuarail, then crosses a deeper gap before the final climb up to the summit plateau of wedge-shaped Aonach Meadhoin, during which it is necessary to put hand to rock.

Continuing westwards from Aonach Meadhoin, the ridge descends and narrows sharply over a rocky section (an easy scramble that the path bypasses) on its way to the next bealach. Note the path along the spur ridge on the left here, which will be your descent route on the return journey. A straightforward ascent then leads to the summit ridge of Sgurr a' Bhealaich

Dheirg, whose highest point is a prominent cairn on the right, reached by a somewhat exposed but easy 70m scramble along the rocky north-east ridge. An unusual feature of this ridge is the dry stone dyke that runs right along its sharp crest.

Returning to the main ridge, the route onwards continues westwards along a broad level shoulder for about 400m before turning left at a cairn and descending steeply to the next bealach. Near the foot of the descent the path zigzags left to avoid an abrupt drop that makes a sporting scramble. One hundred metres further on, another short and easy scramble leads over a hump in the ridge before the bealach is finally reached.

The path then takes a rising traverse around another hump and climbs without incident up the grassy summit slopes of Saileag, whose true summit lies 100m (330ft) beyond the first top reached. To return to your starting point, go back along the ridge to just before the bealach between Sgurr a' Bhealaich Dheirg and Aonach Meadhoin. Branch right from here down a broad ridge leading out to Meall a' Charra, from where views over picturesque Loch Cluanie provide a fitting finish to the day. From the last top on the ridge, descend left around forestry plantations and cross the Allt Coire Tholl Bhruach to rejoin the path along its left bank.

Approaching Sgurr an Fhuarail (centre right) and Aonach Meadhoin (left).

55

	1	2	3	4	5
grade					
terrain					
navigation					
seriousness					

OS MAP: 33
GR: 981223
DISTANCE: 8 miles (13km)
ASCENT: 1,140m (3,750ft)
TIME: 6½ hours

ASSESSMENT: a route of two contrasting halves, beginning with a high plateau walk and ending with a scramble amidst impressive rock scenery.

SEASONAL NOTES: under snow the ascent should pose few problems, although the steep exit from Coire an Sgairne may require care. The ridge to Sgurr a' Choire Ghairbh is a sporting winter route for the experienced only.

'In Kintail everything culminates. Nothing lacks. It is the epitome of the West Highland scene' wrote W H Murray, and there is no better illustration of this than Beinn Fhada, a long complex mountain that is as large as all the Five Sisters put together. It is a mountain of many contrasts, from steep, grassy hillsides on the south to wild crag-girt corries on the north; from vast expanses of plateau in the east to narrow rock ridges in the west. The best circuit of the mountain approaches the summit plateau from the north and returns via the narrow western reaches to show Beinn Fhada in all its moods.

Begin at the Forestry Commission car park at Dorusduain in Strath Croe, at the end of the minor road which leaves the A87 at the head of Loch Duich. Keep right on the Land Rover track to Dorusduain House; just beyond the gate to the house, branch right on a path down to the bridge over the Abhainn Chonaig. On the far side of the river will be found a good path that leads through the narrow confines of Gleann Choinneachain towards Beinn Fhada. Fifteen minutes after crossing the Allt Coire an Sgairne, leave the path at a cairn and follow the good stalkers' path that cuts back right across the hillside into wild Coire an Sgairne and climbs onto the ridge to the right of Meall a' Bhealaich.

Follow the ridge onto the Plaide Mhor, the vast featureless summit plateau of Beinn Fhada, which provides unbeatable navigational practice in adverse weather, and continue to the summit. Beyond lie further tops stretching away

The map shows Strath Croe, Dorusduain, Gleann Choinneachain, Abhainn Chonaig, Morvich, with peaks including Beinn Bhuidhe 490m/1610', Sgurr a' Choire Ghairbh 870m/2860', Coire Chaoil, Coire Gorm, Bealach an t-Sealgaire, Meall an Fhuarain Mhoir 956m/3136', Coire an Sgairne, Bealach an Sgairne, Meall a' Bhealaich 780m/2560', Plaide Mhor, Beinn Fhada 1032m/3385', and Gleann Lichd. Scale shown in kilometre and mile.

56

towards Glen Affric, but few venture onwards for there are more exciting tops to hand on the return journey.

Head back across the Plaide Mhor to the southern rim of Coire an Sgairne and onto Meall an Fhuarain Mhoir, a rounded top beyond which the character of the route changes. A rocky ridge narrows around Coire Gorm and descends to the Bealach an t-Sealgaire. Some handwork is called for, but the only section that causes pause for thought is the ascent from the bealach, where the steep sloping rock requires care (awkward when wet).

Continuing onwards around Coire Chaoil to Sgurr a' Choire Ghairbh it is necessary to negotiate the curious nicks in the ridge that are so conspicuous from below, but there is no difficulty. The rounded knolls between the nicks are curiously known as Faradh Nighean Fhearchair (Farquhar's Daughter's Shrouds).

To return to Dorusduain, descend the steep ridge curving round to Beinn Bhuidhe and go straight over the end, down steep grass slopes among outcrops towards Dorusduain. These last slopes on the route are very steep and require care: in wet weather they are best avoided by descending westwards from Beinn Bhuidhe towards Morvich.

The Coire Gorm ridge from above the Bealach an t-Sealgaire, Beinn Fhada.

Route 25: MAM SODHAIL AND CARN EIGE • THE WESTERN HIGHLANDS

	1	2	3	4	5
grade					
terrain					
navigation					
seriousness					

OS MAP: 25
GR: 200234
DISTANCE: 14 miles (22km)
ASCENT: 1,380m (4,550ft)
TIME: 9 hours

ASSESSMENT: a demanding walk along the twisting and undulating ridges of the spacious Affric hills.

SEASONAL NOTES: a long but entertaining winter route that may have to be curtailed at Carn Eige because of the difficulty of continuing to the

Garbh-bhealach under snow. Glen Affric is at its most colourful in autumn.

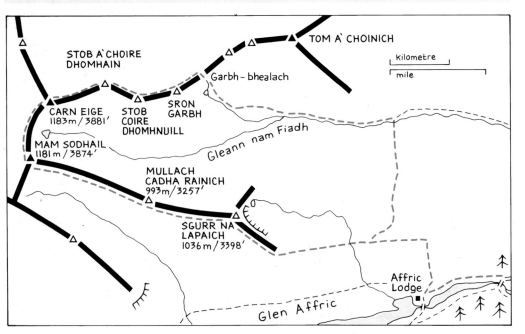

Glen Affric is one of the major showpieces for the integration of hydro-electric power schemes and forestry plantations into the natural environment, and the road along the glen is one of the most scenic in Scotland. Beyond the road-end the long glen forms a major east-west through route past Loch Affric to Kintail. To the north of Loch Affric lies an area of long undulating ridges and high peaks which culminate in the twin summits of Mam Sodhail and Carn Eige, the highest peaks in Britain north of the Great Glen. The traverse of the two mountains around the head of Gleann nam Fiadh makes a strenuous but satisfying high-level tramp, which at one point includes a fine narrow ridge.

Begin at the car park at the end of the public road and take the Land Rover track to Affric Lodge. Just before the lodge a path goes north up the hillside, then west onto the moor beneath Sgurr na Lapaich's craggy east face. Keep to the path until it doubles back away from Sgurr na Lapaich, then head across the moor and climb steep heathery slopes left of the crags to gain the summit. The route onwards is a delightful 2½ mile (4km) length of undulating ridge, narrowing across Mullach Cadha Rainich to the final steep slopes of Mam Sodhail. The huge summit cairn on this, the thirteenth-highest mountain in Britain, testifies to its former importance as a survey point during the OS mapping of the Highlands in the 19th century.

A sharp descent and re-ascent around the head of Gleann nam Fiadh leads to the even higher dome of Carn Eige, from where a side ridge continues northwards to the remote Munro of Beinn Fhionnlaidh. The main route turns eastwards from the summit and descends a broad swathe of ridge that leads to Stob a' Choire Dhomhain and the most interesting section of the whole round. Ahead lies an atypical narrow section of ridge, complete with rock towers, whose crest provides pleasant scrambling; a path bypasses any difficulties. The next two Tops, Stob Coire Dhomhnuill and Sron Garbh, are reached all too soon, but the interest continues as the route descends the remains of a stone staircase on the very crest of the ridge, built by stalkers to ease the descent to the Garbh-bhealach.

Two more Munros wait further along the ridge – Tom a' Choinich and Toll Creagach, but they make an anticlimactic finish to the day; most walkers, like the author, will leave them for next time. From the Garbh-bhealach descend southwards to a lochan in a corrie and follow the left bank of the burn that drains it to pick up a stalkers' path heading down into Gleann nam Fiadh. Follow the path along Gleann nam Fiadh for a little over 1½ miles (2km), then leave it for another that crosses the Abhainn Gleann nam Fiadh and climbs the right bank (left side) of the burn coming down from the moor beneath Sgurr na Lapaich. This rejoins the outward route.

On the ridge from Sgurr na Lapaich to Mam Sodhail.

Route 26: THE MULLARDOCH GROUP • THE WESTERN HIGHLANDS

	1	2	3	4	5
grade					
terrain					
navigation					
seriousness					

OS MAP: 25
GR: 219316
DISTANCE: 17½ miles (28km)
ASCENT: 1,580m (5,200ft)
TIME: 11 hours

ASSESSMENT: a high-level tramp in remote country with far-ranging views.

SEASONAL NOTES: a very long winter's day, especially as the east ridges of An Riabhachan and Sgurr na Lapaich may cause problems under snow. The southern ridges of An Riabhachan's south-west top and Sgurr na Lapaich provide escape routes. Glen Cannich is exceptionally beautiful in the autumn.

North of Glen Affric, beautifully wooded Glen Cannich gives access to the remote mountains lying in the forlorn country between Loch Mullardoch and Loch Monar. Beyond the enormous dam at the road-end, an enlarged Loch Mullardoch has inundated former tracks and the walk along the shore of the loch now has a pioneering feel to it. The four Munros in the interior that await the intrepid mountain walker are worth the effort.

The route begins at the dam with a 5-mile (8km) walk along the north shore of the loch to the stalkers' bothy at the foot of the Allt Socrach (2½ hours). There is a path, which is good in places but frustratingly boggy and undulating in others. Cross the bridge just above the bothy and leave the lochside to take a stalkers' path up the left bank (right side) of the Allt Coire a' Mhaim into Coire Mhaim. When the path ends, keep straight on across the bowl of the corrie and climb the steep grass slopes to gain the crescent-shaped south-east ridge of An Socach, which narrows pleasantly as it curves above deep corries to the summit.

Turning eastwards, the route crosses the deep gap of the Bealach a' Bholla to the first of An Riabhachan's four tops. The ridge narrows again as it zigzags over the second top to provide a long, top-of-the-world stravaig, with Loch Mullardoch on one side and Loch Monar on the other, out to the third top and summit. The fourth top soon follows and then a lovely easy-angled descent leads down the enjoyably narrow east ridge to the Bealach Toll an Lochain.

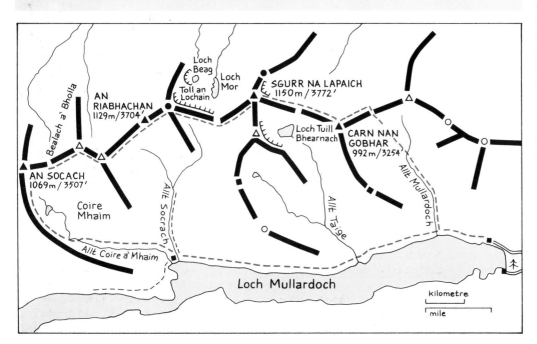

An Riabhachan (left) and Sgurr na Lapaich (centre right) from across Loch Mullardoch.

A stiff pull is now required to gain the summit of Sgurr na Lapaich, from where several fine ridges radiate out around craggy corries. Then things become more interesting again as the route descends the steep east ridge, whose crest is a jumble of huge boulders that call for handwork. A path takes the easiest line, but in mist it is easy to be led down into the corrie on the north; if in doubt, err to the south.

From the broad grassy saddle at the foot of the east ridge, bouldery slopes rise 200m (650ft) to the summit of Carn nan Gobhar, the final Munro of the day. Note that the first cairn you reach is higher than the larger cairn 200m to the south.

Whichever way you choose to descend from the summit, you are going to think there is a better way. Perhaps the best way to avoid the stony hillsides is to descend eastwards to a bealach and then southwards into Coire an t-Sith. Here will be found a stalkers' path that descends the left bank of the Allt Mullardoch to rejoin the lochside path not far from the dam.

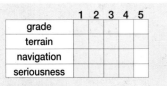

	1	2	3	4	5
grade					
terrain					
navigation					
seriousness					

OS MAP: 25
GR: 958451
DISTANCE: 10 miles (16km)
ASCENT: 910m (3,000ft)
TIME: 7 hours

ASSESSMENT: a tough but absorbing walk around some secret corners of the Coulin deer forest.

SEASONAL NOTES: in winter conditions the steep eastern side of Maol Chean-dearg is best avoided, but an ascent via the south-east ridge should remain practicable, and snow cover may even ease the going.

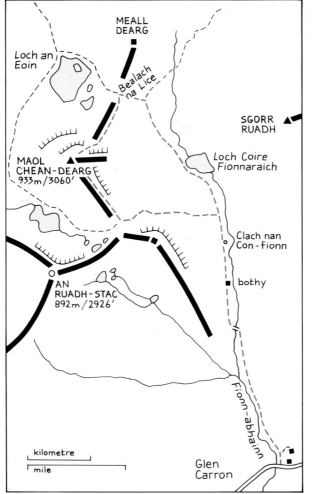

The Coulin deer forest is a complex area of bold, cliff-girt peaks, wild lochans and hidden corners, criss-crossed by a maze of scenic paths that are ideal for backpacking and provide easy access to the interior. Most prominent and intimidating of the Coulin mountains is the isolated bare pate of Maol Chean-dearg, whose ascent from the east penetrates the heart of the area and provides a good test of route-finding abilities on rocky terrain.

Begin at the bridge over the Fionn-abhainn, 5 miles (8km) north-east of Lochcarron village on the A890. Take the track on the right side of the bridge and, at a cattle grid, go left around a fence to join the old path up the broad, heathery glen. After 1½ miles (2km) the path crosses the river (bridge), passes a bothy and reaches the Clach nan Con Fionn, the curious finger of rock to which the legendary Fingal tethered his hounds while hunting. Five hundred metres further on, keep right at a fork to pass the shores of Loch Coire Fionnaraich, then keep left at another fork to reach the Bealach na Lice beneath the east face of Maol Chean-dearg, with the islands of lovely Loch an Eoin spread out below.

Leave the path at the bealach and climb left along the edge of the escarpment overlooking Loch an Eoin to reach the foot of Maol Chean-dearg's craggy north-east face. On closer inspection this face turns out to be less daunting than it looks. According to choice, either (a) ascend the obvious grassy rake (becoming a steep stone shoot) that goes diag-

onally right to reach the skyline at the notch just right of the summit dome, (b) pick a route among outcrops up the open gully that reaches the east ridge to the right of the east buttress, which forms the left-hand skyline, or (c) follow a complex cairned route that goes right and weaves among the crags of the north face. Note, however, that in mist any ascent from this side should be avoided.

The summit dome is isolated from its steep supporting slopes and affords excellent views, especially northwards to the Torridon peaks. Descend via the tough south-east ridge, on awkward boulders at first and then over a section of shattered quartzite, tilted sharply upwards by folding. On the bealach between Maol Chean-dearg and An Ruadh-stac nestles one of the most beautiful lochans in the

Maol Chean-dearg (centre right) from Sgorr Ruadh.

Highlands, its white quartzite walls giving it the appearance of a swimming pool. Only the most dedicated will continue beyond it and make the steep stony ascent of An Ruadh-stac. Most, like the author, will settle for the stalkers' path that descends from the bealach to rejoin the path along the Fionn-abhainn.

	1	2	3	4	5
grade					
terrain					
navigation					
seriousness					

OS MAP: 25
GR: 005484
DISTANCE: 9½ miles (15km)
ASCENT: 1,640m (5,400ft)
TIME: 9 hours

ASSESSMENT: a skyline round of an extensive corrie, with some memorably awkward terrain, but equally memorable situations and scenery.

SEASONAL NOTES: a fine winter ridge walk of exceptional length, which may give considerable problems in some sections. The route can be curtailed half-way round at the Bealach Coire Lair.

The majority of the high peaks of the Coulin deer forest rim the extensive basin of Coire Lair, whose skyline provides the finest and toughest expedition in the area. The corrie's vast, brooding spaciousness is perhaps best appreciated under lowering skies. Begin at the road to Achnashellach station on the A890 and walk up to the station. The excellent path to Coire Lair begins at a stile 130m left along the track, just beyond the grounds of the station house. It climbs into Coire Lair through woods and rhododendron bushes, above gorges studded with waterfalls and gnarled pines.

Once into Coire Lair, keep right at a first fork then right again at a second to reach the bealach south-east of Beinn Liath Mhor, then climb steep slopes of heather and boulders to gain the south-east top. The main summit lies 1½ miles (2km) distant along a ridge of alternating quartzite and sandstone, which is quite narrow in parts – especially at one point along the edge of a buttress overlooking Coire Lair. The quartzite at the summit is purgatorially sharp, but the views of Liathach and Beinn Eighe are without comparison.

Continuing around the corrie skyline, the descent to the Bealach Coire Lair is complicated by lines of cliffs and a craggy knoll that guards the jaws of the bealach. The best line keeps to the crest of the ridge to reach the knoll, then descends left around it to reach the bealach. Gain the north ridge of Sgorr Ruadh by a grassy depression, which tends right beneath outcrops, and scramble up to the tapering summit. A rough descent leads down to the Bealach Mhoir, a long complex bealach studded with sparkling lochans. On a hot day it is entirely possible that you may not wish to continue beyond here, especially as a path descends from here to rejoin the Coire Lair path.

The next mountain on the round, however, is Fuar Tholl which, with its peculiarly scalloped hillsides and awesome Mainreachan Buttress, is the finest mountain in the area. Climb its northern slopes directly, easily breaching a band of cliffs half-way up, and cross the top of the Mainreachan Buttress to reach the summit. On the way, pause to view the buttress, which contains some of the best sandstone climbs in the country.

Continuing over towards Achnashellach from the summit, you are immediately confronted with the cliff edge of the deep-cut south-east corrie. Descend the interesting left-hand rim, which is quite sharp and exposed near the top, though of no technical difficulty. When the ridge levels off, cut down right to the lochan in the corrie, then aim directly for the junction of the River Lair and the railway line. The long descent through boulder-strewn heather is as tough as they come. If river conditions permit, it is better to cross to the path on the left bank.

Beinn Liath Mhor from the Bealach Coire Lair.

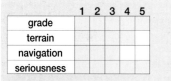

	1	2	3	4	5
grade					
terrain					
navigation					
seriousness					

OS MAP: 24
GR: 869577
DISTANCE: 6 miles (10km)
ASCENT: 1,190m (3,900ft)
TIME: 6½ hours

ASSESSMENT: a good introduction to Torridonian 'hillwalking' on a mountain full of fascinating features, with all hard scrambling avoidable, if necessary.

SEASONAL NOTES: the traverse of the Horns is a major winter mountaineering expedition.

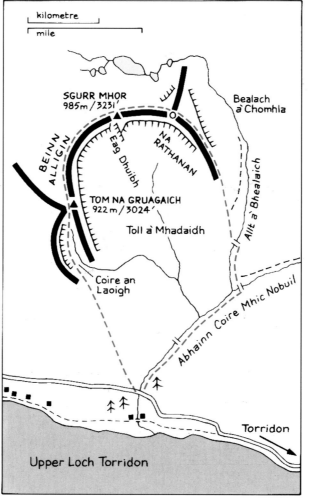

Glen Torridon is one of the scenic gems of the Northern Highlands. Its austere beauty and majestic, sculptured sandstone peaks impose themselves upon the imagination. The Torridonian mountains are often regarded as the oldest in the world (the sandstone from which they were formed is over 1,000 million years old), and there is certainly something primeval about their bulky shapes crouching on the moor like prehistoric monsters.

The three major peaks on the north side of Glen Torridon (Routes 29-31) exhibit all that is characteristic of walking in the area: rough approaches, narrow ridges, exhilarating scrambling and superb situations. Beinn Alligin is the most westerly and least complex of the three peaks. When viewed across Upper Loch, Torridon is seen to consist of three tops, two of which demand a closer look, the centre top being split by the enormous gash of the Eag Dhuibh, and the right-hand top consisting of three rocky prongs – the famous Rathanan or Horns of Alligin. A closer look is guaranteed not to disappoint.

Begin on the minor road from Torridon to Diabeg, at the car park by the bridge over the Abhainn Coire Mhic Nobuil. Take the path through the pines on the left bank (right side) of the gorge; ignore the boggy path that branches left after 15 minutes. Beyond the confluence with the Allt a' Bhealaich, the path crosses the river (bridge) and forks. Keep left along the left bank (right side) of the Allt a' Bhealaich, following a path that crosses to the

right bank (bridge) and continues to the Bealach a' Chomhla right of Beinn Alligin. Leave the path to climb the ridge rising up to the Horns.

The traverse of the Horns is an exciting scramble, but the delights of the exposed sandstone terraces will not be appreciated by all. Those who prefer not to have their hair raised will be pleased to note that the Horns can be bypassed on steep grass slopes to the left.

Beyond the Horns a steep, narrow ridge leads to the summit of Sgurr Mhor, Beinn Alligin's highest top. Continuing round Toll a' Mhadaidh, the ridge broadens past the edge of the Eag Dhuibh. This remarkable cleft plunges 550m (1,800ft) into the corrie, where its boulder debris makes for interesting exploration but purgatorial going. Beyond a dip, the ridge narrows again to the summit of Tom na Gruagaich (a new

Beinn Alligin from the path to Beinn Damh.

Munro in 1997), perched high above the precipices of Toll a' Mhadaidh. From the dip to the west of the summit, descend into Coire an Laoigh, following the burn down out of the corrie and then aiming back across the moor (cairned) to your starting point.

Route 30: LIATHACH • THE NORTHERN HIGHLANDS

	1	2	3	4	5
grade					
terrain					
navigation					
seriousness					

OS MAP: 25
GR: 936567
DISTANCE: 6 miles (10km)
ASCENT: 1,340m (4,400ft)
TIME: 7½ hours

ASSESSMENT: a spectacular and thrilling scramble, with some fine situations and lots of atmosphere.

SEASONAL NOTES: the whole route is a major winter mountaineering expedition.

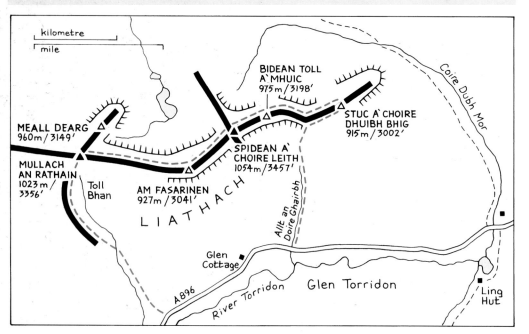

There are few more imposing sights in Scotland than the primeval bulk of Liathach rising fortress-like above Glen Torridon. Its steep terraced slopes appear impregnable from below, but can be breached at either end to give access to a sensational ridge whose traverse constitutes one of the most spectacular scrambles on the mainland.

Begin about 700m east of Glen Cottage bunkhouse in Glen Torridon, at the bridge over the Allt an Doire Ghairbh, taking the path on the left bank (right side) of the burn that climbs steeply up the craggy hillside into a small corrie. Higher up, care is required as the rough path negotiates some steep, rocky ground to debouch onto the main ridge at the bealach west of Stuc a' Choire Dhuibh Bhig. It is worth making the short detour to the summit of the Stuc for the view of Beinn Eighe (Route 31) before turning westwards along the ridge.

As far as Spidean a' Choire Leith (Liathach's highest summit), the narrowest section of ridge remains hidden, but the immediate prospect ahead is impressive enough, with the narrow quartzite ridge curving round above the great sandstone buttresses of Coire Leith. The stony ridge begins with a stroll around the corrie to the foot of Bidean Toll a' Mhuic, then ascends more steeply over the twin tops of that peak to the summit of Spidean a' Choire Leith.

A 150m (500ft) descent down Spidean's stony south-west slopes (confusing in mist) leads to a short, level, grassy section that heralds the onset of the most exciting scramble of the day – the traverse of the pinnacled crest of Am Fasarinen. A good head for heights is required, one section having to be taken *à cheval*, but most of the 'difficulties' can be avoided by following a track lower down on the south side, if necessary. The situation and the exposure are spectacular.

Beyond the pinnacles, a pleasant stroll leads onto Mullach an Rathain, the last top of the day and a fine perch from which to contemplate the beautiful western seascape. To the north, the pinnacles of the north ridge beckon towards Meall Dearg, but they are best left to those with rock climbing experience.

From the Mullach, the most interesting descent to the glen is via the south-west ridge, which provides an entertaining scramble near the top and, if a direct line is taken, a breathtaking aerial view of Torridon village.

When the ridge veers south-east, cut left into the Toll Bhan and follow the stream down; to avoid all scrambling on the descent, descend into the Toll directly from the south-west ridge. The day ends with a short walk back along the glen to your starting point.

The pinnacles of Am Fasarinen, Liathach.

	1	2	3	4	5
grade					
terrain					
navigation					
seriousness					

OS MAP: 19/25
GR: 977578
DISTANCE: 12 miles (19km)
ASCENT: 1,280m (4,200ft)
TIME: 9 hours

ASSESSMENT: a memorable ridge walk and scramble amidst awesome scenery.

SEASONAL NOTES: in winter the narrow ridges and steep hillsides of Beinn Eighe require technical competence; the descent of the Ceum Grannda is for experts only.

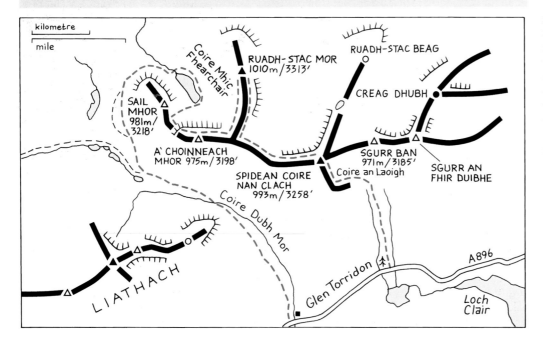

The sprawling scree-girt mass of Beinn Eighe is a complex mountain range in miniature, which contains seven peaks over 914m (3,000ft), strung out along narrow quartzite ridges. The main ridge extends for 3 miles (5km) along the north side of Glen Torridon and gives the mountain its name. The route described here explores the western end of the mountain, where magnificent Coire Mhic Fhearchair lies hidden far from the road between ridges that provide rewarding scrambling.

Begin 5 miles (8km) towards Glen Torridon from Kinlochewe, where a path passes to the right of a small plantation of trees and climbs into Coire an Laoigh (parking 100m west). Once into the corrie, bear left onto its bounding rocky east ridge and scramble around the corrie skyline and up shifting quartzite slopes to reach the main ridge 200m west of Spidean Coire nan Clach (a new Munro in 1997).

From here the route goes west along the main ridge, but first scramble to the summit of Spidean Coire nan Clach and, if time and energy permit, continue eastwards across a dip and a pleasant, level and boulder-strewn section, to Sgurr Ban to view the Black Carls – the pinnacles at the eastern end of the ridge.

Heading westwards from Spidean Coire nan Clach, the main ridge reaches the grassy summit plateau of A' Choinneach Mhor at the head of Coire Mhic Fhearchair. This corrie is one of the scenic wonders of Scotland, its 300m (1,00ft) Triple Buttresses providing an awesome backdrop to a sparkling lochan.

Before continuing to the summit of A' Choinneach Mhor at the west end of the plateau, cross the saddle to the north around the rim of the corrie and ascend Ruadh Stac Mor, Beinn Eighe's highest peak.

From the saddle, a stone shoot can be descended into the corrie, but a much better route for the fit and capable is to return to A' Choinneach Mhor's summit plateau and climb the short distance to the summit at the edge of the Triple Buttresses. Continuing over the top towards Sail Mhor, the Ceum Grannda (meaning 'ugly step') is encountered. No place less deserves its name, for its lovely clean slabs of rock provide engrossing scrambling, giving one a flavour of the exposed climbing on the Triple Buttresses. The last few metres are probably best descended facing inwards. All difficulties can be avoided on the left. Continue over a rocky knob to the foot of Sail Mhor's

The Triple Buttresses of Coire Mhic Fearchair, Beinn Eighe.

south-east ridge and descend grass slopes into Coire Mhic Fearchair. A path leads round the lochan, from where the view of the Triple Buttresses is unforgettable.

The path continues down into Coire Mhic Nobuill and reaches the roadside 1½ miles (2km) from your starting point.

	1	2	3	4	5
grade					
terrain					
navigation					
seriousness					

OS MAP: 19
GR: 114850
DISTANCE: 16 miles (25km)
ASCENT: 1,530m (5,050ft)
TIME: 10½ hours

ASSESSMENT: a long approach and steep ascent to the classically-shaped summit ridge of a magnificent hidden mountain.

SEASONAL NOTES: the steep slopes of Beinn Dearg Mhor can be dangerous under snow or when iced.

Note: Beinn Dearg Mhor is named Beinn Dearg Mor on the current OS map.

Although hidden behind and overshadowed by its striking neighbour An Teallach (route 33), Beinn Dearg Mhor is a compelling mountain in its own right. It has a magnificent setting above the hidden mountain fastness of Srath na Sealga and has a unique purity of line, consisting almost entirely of a crescent-shaped ridge that encloses the deeply sculptured and exquisitely proportioned Coire nan Clach. The experienced mountaineer W H Murray noted that he had 'never seen a corrie more shapely'. The approach to the mountain is long, but the rewards are commensurate.

Begin at the lay-by 100m south of the bridge over the Allt Gleann Chaorachain on the A832 2 miles (4km) south of Dundonnell. A cart track heads south up the glen through beautiful mixed woodland on the east side of the river, then crosses the river to a high point on the moor beneath the pinnacled ridges of An Teallach. One hundred metres beyond the high point, branch right on a path that contours round An Teallach's south-east shoulder to descend to the lonely Shenavall bothy on the flats of Srath na Sealga, near the head of Loch na Sealga.

Across the strath Beinn Dearg Mhor is an irresistible attraction, but reaching its foot is not easy; there is no way to keep feet dry here. First, ford the Abhainn Srath na Sealga below Shenavall, then follow the river beside some extremely marshy ground to the Abhainn Gleann na Muice and ford this second river close to Larachantivore cottage. Both rivers are

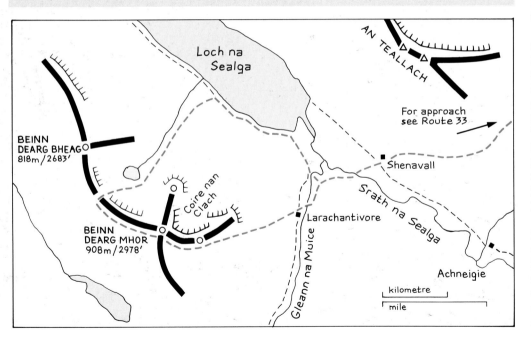

wide and, when in spate, impassable. Climb the steep earthy rake left of the north-east ridge of Beinn Dearg Mhor to reach the east top. The ridge itself offers scrambling opportunities and is worth exploring, although in places it is exposed and vegetated.

From the east top, follow the rim of Coire nan Clach round behind an impressive overhanging prow to the main summit, a lonely eyrie in the wilderness that has a unique aura of solitude. The rocky ridge that forms the western arm of the corrie narrows to a castellated north top and is well worth investigation, but there is no way off the end.

The route onwards from the main summit goes westwards for a short distance, then descends north-westwards down steep, earthy slopes to the bealach below Beinn Dearg Bheag. Climb Beinn Dearg Bheag if you have time, for its summit ridge is exhilaratingly narrow, with a succession of rocky tops leading north-westwards towards Gruinard Bay.

From the bealach, descend grassy rakes between cliffs (great care required in mist) to reach Loch Toll an Lochain, whose sandy shores may well tempt you to tarry awhile at the thought of what still lies ahead – merely a tough descent to Loch na Sealga, more river crossings and the long walk out from Shenavall.

Beinn Dearg Mhor from Shenavall.

	1	2	3	4	5
grade					
terrain					
navigation					
seriousness					

OS MAP: 19
GR: 111858
DISTANCE: 8½ miles (14km)
ASCENT: 1,450m (4,750ft)
TIME: 8 hours

ASSESSMENT: a thrilling scramble on one of the most spectacular of all Scottish mountains.

SEASONAL NOTES: the traverse of An Teallach's crest is a major winter mountaineering expedition.

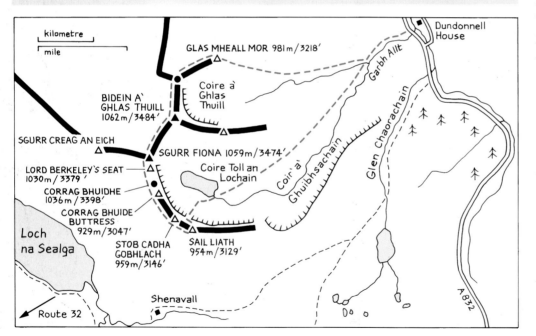

An Teallach is an awesome, pinnacled wedge of old red sandstone regarded by many as the finest peak in Scotland. When struck red by the rays of the setting sun, or when mists curl like smoke around its pinnacles, it admirably suits its evocative Gaelic name meaning 'The Forge'.

It has much in common with the sandstone peaks of Torridon to the south, and if taken direct, the traverse of the sharp summit ridge is harder than any of these, involving some sensational situations on a succession of rock towers. For those of a more nervous disposition, a path contours round most of the more awkward sections. Top tickers will have much work to do here, as besides two Munros, there are no less than a further eight Tops that are listed in Munro's Tables.

The finest features of An Teallach's complex topography are the two eastern corries (Coire a' Ghlas Thuill and Toll an Lochain) and the ridges that enclose them; the best route on the mountain makes a circuit of their skylines. Begin at the foot of the Garbh Allt near Dundonnell House on the A832 and follow the left bank (right side) of the stream. Cross another branch of the stream after a short distance, then follow a clearing on the right around rhododendron thickets to pick up a good path on the riverbank. At the confluence with the burn coming down from Coire a' Ghlas Thuill, keep right to follow that burn up into the corrie, then leave it and climb steep slopes directly to the summit of Glas Mheall Mor. There follows a pleasant stroll round the corrie rim to a small top before the final 180m (590ft) haul up Bidein a' Ghlas Thuill, An Teallach's highest point. From here a steep descent and re-ascent of 150m (500ft) leads to Sgurr Fiona, the second of An Teallach's two Munros.

The view ahead from Sgurr Fiona brings to mind Pennant's 1772 description of An Teallach: 'horrible and awful with summits broken, sharp and serrated and springing into all terrific forms'. The first rock tower is Lord Berkeley's Seat, an easy scramble over sandstone terraces; it can be bypassed on the right, but should be ascended for the vertiginous view over the edge to Loch Toll an Lochain. Next come the Corrag Bhuidhe pinnacles, hard, airy scrambles that can again be avoided on the right, and Corrag Bhuidhe Buttress. To avoid the descent at the end of Corrag Bhuidhe Buttress, on which walkers have fallen to their deaths, follow the path out right to a short, exposed scramble where care is required.

The rest of the ridge develops into a pleasant walk, rising again to Stob Cadha Gobhlach, then crossing Cadha Gobhlach to end on Sail Liath. Descend by returning to the first of the two gullies of Cadha Gobhlach and going down into Toll an Lochain, pausing by the lochside to admire the surrounding cliffs. From the corrie easy going over a quartzite escarpment leads back down Coir' a' Ghuibhsachain to your starting point.

The southern tops of An Teallach from Sgurr Fiona.

	1	2	3	4	5
grade					
terrain					
navigation					
seriousness					

OS MAP: 15
GR: 139066
DISTANCE: 9½ miles (15km)
ASCENT: 1,020m (3,350ft)
TIME: 6½ hours

ASSESSMENT: a rough walk amidst stunning rock scenery and coastal views.

SEASONAL NOTES: in winter the gully beside the prow of the Fiddler becomes a steep snow climb, and the Garbh Choireachan ridge may also require care.

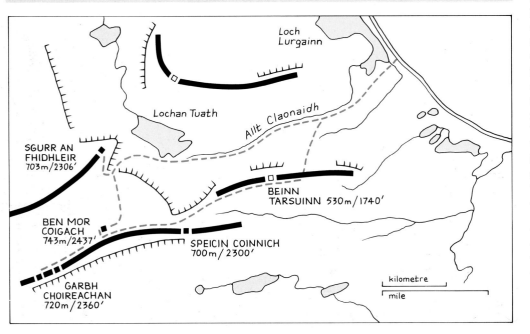

In the north-west corner of Ross and Cromarty, jutting out into the Minch, lies the district of Coigach. It is an area of shattered sandstone peaks rearing in dramatic isolation above desolate moorlands of bog and lochan. Although the hills are not high by Scottish standards, they provide spectacular walking, and none more so than the breathtaking summits of Sgurr an Fhidleir and Ben Mor Coigach.

Begin 2 miles (3km) along the minor road that leaves the A835 at Drumrunie junction 9 miles (15km) north of Ullapool. Cross the river below the road, about 100m east of where it enters Loch Lurgainn (stepping stones), and make for the right bank (left side) of the Allt Claonaidh. An attempt at a path climbs beside the river, which forms some fine pools and cascades, but the going is very boggy. Follow the course of the river to Lochan Tuath at the foot of the impressive prow of the Fiddler. When viewed across the sandy bays of the loch this awesome wedge of rock, unique in Scotland, has an air of impregnability and unreality; not until 1962 was it climbed direct, and you may be forgiven for wondering how it was ever climbed at all.

The walkers' route to the summit goes up the obvious steep heather gully to the left of the prow; use sheep tracks to ease the going. The gully debouches onto the plateau between the Fiddler and Ben Mor Coigach, and easy boulder slopes on the right lead up to the Fiddler's summit. With care, steep grass slopes on the right can be descended to the top of the prow for a spectacular view of Lochan Tuath 430m beneath your feet. Later in the day the shadow of the Fiddler's prow steals across the lochan as though devouring it.

To reach Ben Mor Coigach, retrace your steps to the plateau and climb easy grass slopes to the summit; in adverse weather good navigation is required here. From the summit a 1 mile (1½km) long narrow ridge beckons seawards to the twin tops of the Garbh Choireachan, with tremendous views southwards over Loch Broom and westwards over the Summer Isles to the Minch and the Outer Hebrides. Small rock towers that stand astride the ridge provide pleasant diversions if you want some scrambling practice, but they are easily bypassed on the north side.

From the Garbh Choireachan, retrace your steps along the ridge, bypassing the summit of Ben Mor Coigach and continuing as far as the bealach before Speicin Coinnich (which can be climbed by a short scramble). Descend open slopes below the bealach towards Beinn Tarsuinn and climb to its summit for a classic view of the Fiddler. Continue over the summit and descend a few hundred metres to a level section of ridge; at the end of this, head directly down steep heather slopes, circumventing one or two outcrops, to reach the Allt Claonaidh and the route of ascent.

The Garbh Choireachan from Ben Mor Coigach.

	1	2	3	4	5
grade					
terrain					
navigation					
seriousness					

OS MAP: 15
GR: 107095
DISTANCE: 2 miles (3km)
ASCENT: 560m (1,850ft)
TIME: 3 hours

ASSESSMENT: a scrambler's paradise on pinnacled ridges high above the wilds of Assynt.

SEASONAL NOTES: in rare winter conditions the ascent route may become a steep snow slope and the summit ridge requires great care when iced.

'Then the sun came out and the traverse of the ridge from end to end was sheer delight. There is nothing like it in all Britain, for it consists of a succession of little needles and pinnacles with lateral ridges sticking out on either side, and whose grotesque appearance baffles description.'

BEN HUMBLE (*On Scottish Hills*, 1946)

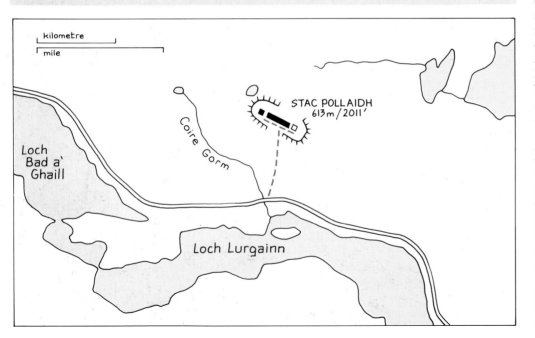

Stac Pollaidh is the smallest mountain in this book, less than half the height of some, but it is a perfect mountain in miniature and what it lacks in stature it more than makes up for in character. Its soaring wedge shape rises in splendid isolation from the surrounding moorland, making it seem much higher than it is. The traverse of its prickly sandstone summit ridge calls for some tricky manoeuvres amidst spectacular rock scenery.

There is a wide choice of routes up to the summit ridge, but the main interest begins once you are up there, above the apron of scree that surrounds the mountain, so the shortest way up is as good as any. Begin at the car park at the bridge over the burn coming down from Coire Gorm, 5 miles (8km) along the minor road from Drumrunie junction on the A835. Climb the very steep earthy path which, making no concessions to contouring, takes a *directissima* route up the grassy hillside to the low point on the summit ridge. Height is gained fast on Stac Pollaidh, and it shouldn't take much more than an hour to gain the summit ridge.

Turn right to visit the east top first, scrambling on sloping sandstone ledges across a notch, which many will prefer to bypass on a path lower down. Now re-cross the notch and make your way westwards to the higher western top. The complex ridge bristles with weird pinnacles and towers, like the splintered ruins of an ancient fortress. A maze of paths provides endless choices of route, easy or spectacular depending on inclination and imagination.

Scrambling of all grades can be sought or avoided almost altogether, and spur ridges can be explored. Some of the sandstone formations are loose and require care, but for the most part the scrambling is wonderfully entertaining and most will find the ridge not nearly long enough. Note especially the second gully from the end (Pinnacle Basin), which contains the peculiar Lobster's Claw among other fantastic formations. The views are superb, especially northwards over a patchwork of land and water to the sharp summit ridge of Suilven (Route 36).

Guarding the summit stands one unavoidable barrier: a rock tower that must be climbed direct. It is easier than it looks, with good ledges for feet and a good jug handle half-way up, but the exposure and the prospect of having to reverse it dissuade many. Perhaps more expletives are uttered here than on any other Scottish mountain. To descend, return to the low point on the ridge to regain the roadside.

Stac Pollaidh from Sgurr An Fhidleir.

	1	2	3	4	5
grade					
terrain					
navigation					
seriousness					

OS MAP: 15
GR: 107220
DISTANCE: 13 miles (21km)
ASCENT: 880m (2,900ft)
TIME: 8 hours

ASSESSMENT: an attractive approach and an exciting ridge scramble on Scotland's striking Pillar Mountain.

SEASONAL NOTES: a major winter mountaineering expedition, when even the stone shoot may become a steep snow climb.

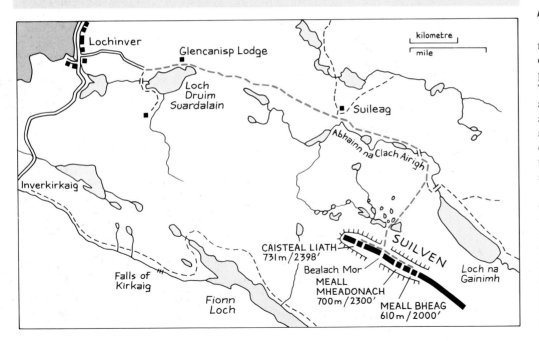

'More than a hundred lochs and lochans lie around. When the sky is bright they scintillate, brilliantly blue, and all about them wild hills rise stark. When the sky is heavy, and grey mists twist among the mountain spires, they glint whitely or lie black and fathomless. The scene is never without beauty, weird or brilliant as the skies dictate.'

*W H MURRAY on the view from Suilven
(Highland Landscape, 1962)*

The striking sandstone peak of Suilven rises boldly above the lochan-studded Sutherland moors like an impregnable monolith, its formidable western buttress as seen from Lochinver prompting the Vikings to name it Pillar Mountain. To the Gaels it became known as the Grey Castle, and more recently the Sugar Loaf. Despite its apparent unscalability, the 1 mile (1½km) long summit ridge is easily reached by stone shoots on either side, but the traverse of the three sharp tops is a more exciting affair, calling for careful and exposed scrambling in superb situations.

The best approach is from the road to Glencanisp Lodge, which leaves the A837 at the south end of Lochinver. Begin 1 mile (2km) along at the end of the public road, where there is a parking space. Continue along the road and through the grounds of the lodge, beyond which the track descends to a fork at the end of Loch Druim Suardalain. Branch left here on an excellent well-drained stalkers' path that strikes eastwards towards Suilven, undulating alongside a chain of lochans among rock outcrops typical of gneissian Sutherland terrain.

Keep right at a cairned fork near Suileag to draw slowly alongside the north face of Suilven, which from here has the appearance of a beached galleon. The access stone shoot can be seen leading up to the lowest point on the ridge (the Bealach Mor). About 600m after the path crosses the Abhainn na Clach Airigh, branch right on a side path that crosses the moorland to a shelf of attractive lochans and climbs steeply up the stone shoot. At the Bealach Mor, turn right for an easy but exposed scramble to the table-top summit of Caisteal Liath, for a great view of the western seascape.

The two eastern tops are trickier than Caisteal Liath, but are well worth exploring if you feel capable. Return to the Bealach Mor and scramble up Meall Mheadonach, avoiding some awkward towers by a path on the right, if necessary. The top is surprisingly level and grassy, but soon drops steeply to a narrow bealach from where the climb up Meall Bheag is the most sensational on the ridge, requiring exposed scrambling on loose rocky terraces. Keep left to find the easiest line, and remember that you will have to reverse it.

The return route is as for the approach. On a hot summer's day the shelf of lochans at the foot of the stone shoot is a seductive place to recuperate before the long walk out.

The summit ridge of Suilven from Casteal Liath.

	1	2	3	4	5
grade					
terrain					
navigation					
seriousness					

OS MAP: 15
GR: 251218
DISTANCE: 11½ miles (18km)
ASCENT: 1,130m (3,700ft)
TIME: 7½ hours

ASSESSMENT: an unusual route across startling changes of terrain on Assynt's highest mountains.

SEASONAL NOTES: in winter the connecting ridge between the summit and south top of Ben More Assynt should be tackled by experienced mountaineers only; others should descend by the route of ascent.

Conival and Ben More Assynt are the crowning hills of the Sutherland district of Assynt, an area of great geological and historical interest. The name Assynt is probably derived from a Norse word meaning rocky and, if so, these two mountains are worthy representatives of the area, for their connecting ridge sports an enormous collection of quartzite stones, more like a beach than a mountain top.

The circuit of the two mountains passes through an absorbing variety of rock scenery, from limestone caves to shattered quartzite summits and a narrow gneiss ridge, which calls for some sporting scrambling in parts.

Begin near Inchnadamph Hotel on the A837, taking the private road along the right bank of the River Traligill to Glenbain Cottage. A path continues beyond the cottage, crossing the river and passing the Cnoc nan Uamh cave system, whose underground river can easily be reached beneath an arched cave entrance (both torch and care required). The whole area is rich in caves and is still yielding new finds; some of the caves have revealed the earliest traces of human habitation in Scotland, dating from around 6,000 BC.

Leave the path to follow the course of the River Traligill up Gleann Dubh, taking time to explore the limestone riverbed of this Giant's Ravine as you go, then aim diagonally up the grassy south-west slopes of Beinn an Fhurain to reach the bealach between it and Conival. A further stiff 250m (820ft) climb over shattered quartzite leads to the summit of Conival.

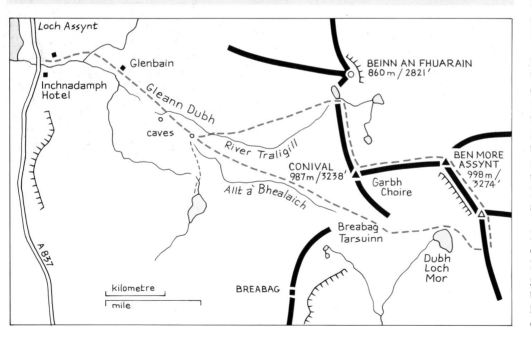

The summit of Ben More Assynt lies 1 mile (1½ km) to the east across a broad ridge of similar shattered quartzite. The terrain is featureless, almost surreal, and in mist it can be difficult to distinguish the summit from any other heap of stones. At the summit the route turns south-eastwards, leaving the quartzite behind for a ridge of more reliable gneiss, the oldest rock in the world, here reaching a greater height than anywhere else in Scotland.

Above Dubh Loch More the ridge narrows to a sharp arête, which has been flatteringly compared to Aonach Eagach (Route 10), with several awkward moves across exposed slabs requiring care, particularly when wet.

The ridge leads to the south top of Ben More Assynt, from where there is a good view of the fine Garbh Coire of Conival cupped high beneath the summit. About 500m beyond the south top, a way can be made down

Ben More Assynt summit (left centre) and south top (right) from the south ridge.

towards Dubh Loch Mor, steeply at first but becoming easier lower down. To return to your starting point, make for the narrow defile between Conival and Breabag Tarsuinn, which leads to a descent by the Allt a' Bhealaich into Gleann Dubh.

	1	2	3	4	5
grade					
terrain					
navigation					
seriousness					

ASSESSMENT: a very undulating ridge walk, narrow in parts, across the many tops of an odd-shaped mountain.

OS MAP: 15
GR: 232274
DISTANCE: 8 miles (13km)
ASCENT: 1,040m (3,400ft)
TIME: 6 hours

SEASONAL NOTES: under snow or ice many sections of the ridge require great care and are not for the inexperienced.

'This (ledge) rises sharply, and on it are some large blocks of rock which have to be swarmed over and none are too secure... The leader could not get enough purchase off the heather to make the ascent, so stones were passed up to him to enable him to do so... The last man has to kick off and be pulled up. After this the climbing is sensational.'

HAROLD RAEBURN describing the first ascent of the Barrel Buttress of Sail Gharbh in 1907.

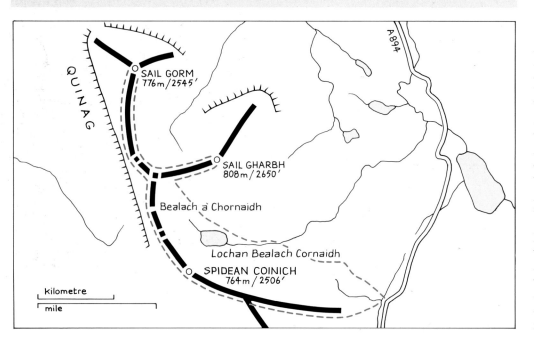

Quinag is the most northerly of the chain of great sandstone peaks that rise in the north-west of Scotland. It is a peculiar 'Y' shaped mountain that looks different from every bend in the roads that almost encircle it. From Kylesku to the north, the barrel-shaped buttresses of the two northern 'heels' of the 'Y' are particularly impressive. The entire mountain consists of six tops linked by ridges that are narrow in parts but nowhere difficult. The drops between the tops are of sufficient depth to test resolve in bagging them all, but the complete traverse makes an exhilarating tramp amidst typically spacious Assynt scenery.

Begin on the A894, 4 miles (7km) north of Inchnadamph, just around a right-hand bend where there is a large parking space on the east side of the road and a stalkers' path on the west. Aim directly across the moor to the foot of the south-east ridge of Spidean Coinich. A cairned path ascends the edge of the escarpment, which becomes increasingly steep and boulder-strewn as height is gained. From the summit there is a fine view over Loch Assynt to Conival (Route 37), and to the north Foinaven (Route 39) is prominent.

The most interesting section of the route now begins, with a short, sharp descent to a narrow level ridge, followed by another steep descent to an enticing lochan. From here, grass slopes lead up to a sharp top, and then a path goes straight down the narrow crest of the twisting north-west ridge to the Bealach a' Chornaidh.

Another steep ascent on grass leads to the centre top of Quinag at the junction of the two heels of the 'Y'; a rock band, half-way up, is easily avoided on the right. The two heels can now be visited in turn. Begin with the ascent of Sail Gorm to the north, which first involves the negotiation of a bold rocky hump that bars the way; steep but straightforward. Then follows a long climb along a gentle ridge, at one point passing along the edge of a spectacular buttress, to reach the eyrie of Sail Gorm, from where the view of the western seaboard is mesmerising.

Make the return trip to the centre top, re-negotiating the rocky hump, and cross a short dip to Quinag's other heel and highest top, Sail Gharbh. To descend, return to the dip and go down steep grass slopes to pick up the cairned stalkers' path that crosses the flat moor left of Lochan Bealach Cornaidh which leads back to your starting point.

Climbing Spidean Coinich, Quinag.

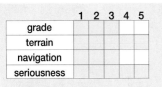 

	1	2	3	4	5
grade					
terrain					
navigation					
seriousness					

OS MAP: 9
GR: 307565
DISTANCE: 14 miles (22km)
ASCENT: 1,280m (4,200ft)
TIME: 9 hours

ASSESSMENT: an engrossing walk along the shattered ridges of a crumbling mountain.

SEASONAL NOTES: in the right winter conditions beautiful snow arêtes form along the ridge, but their traverse should not be attempted by the inexperienced.

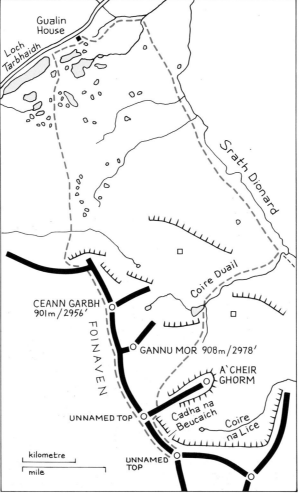

In the desolate wastes of north-west Sutherland the shattered quartzite peak of Foinaven dominates a wild and savagely indifferent landscape pitted with water. The traverse of the long summit ridge is an exceptionally interesting expedition, although the remote and disintegrating nature of the terrain can be an unsettling experience.

Park just over the brow of the hill beyond Gualin House on the A838 4½ miles (7km) north of Rhiconich, where a gate in the fence gives access to the Land Rover track up Srath Dionard. Begin here, or a short distance back along the road, and cross the moor left of Loch Tarbhaidh, patiently threading your way through the maze of bog and lochan that obstructs the approach to Foinaven's north-west shoulder. With relief, negotiate the craggy slopes onto the shoulder and climb uniform boulder slopes to the summit of Ceann Garbh, Foinaven's most northerly top.

A path leads off along the summit ridge, initially narrow and stony, but soon broadening to provide a delightful grassy stroll, with superlative views on either side. Leaving the greenery behind for good, the ridge curves upwards in a perfect arc to Gannu Mor, Foinaven's highest summit. Note in mist that the high point lies beyond the first cairn reached, at the end of a short ridge jutting eastwards. From the first cairn, descend onto a level section of ridge that narrows over a short rise and down to a bealach, then climb more steeply to an unnamed top above A' Cheir Ghorm.

The return route descends towards A' Cheir Ghorm, but first follow the main ridge around Coire na Lice, amidst the most spectacular scenery of the day. The ridge narrows across the prominent buttress, known as Lord Reay's Seat, to reach the Cadha na Beucaich, where a pinnacle astride the ridge is easily bypassed. The ridge then climbs to another unnamed top above some of the remotest cliffs in Britain, whose full climbing potential was not realised until the 1960s.

Returning to the top above A' Cheir Ghorm, descend the steep east ridge to the bealach between these two tops. It is worth wandering out along the shattered ridge to the end point of A' Cheir Ghorm (with some exposed scrambling in places if the crest is adhered to) for the perspective on the main ridge and the eerie sound of falling quartzite as the mountain disintegrates around you.

From the bealach, descend mobile slopes on the north side (please leave some mountain behind for the next person) and follow the river down between cliffs into Coire Duail. Continue down beside the river into remote and forlorn Srath Dionard to meet the Land Rover track that leads all the way back to Gualin House.

A'Cheir Ghorm from the misty main ridge of Foinaven.

	1	2	3	4	5
grade					
terrain					
navigation					
seriousness					

OS MAP: 43/44
GR: 186911
DISTANCE: 12 miles (19km)
ASCENT: 910m (3,000ft)
TIME: 7½ hours

ASSESSMENT: a beautiful woodland walk and rock scramble lead to one of the great corries of the Scottish Highlands.

SEASONAL NOTES: the north-east corrie is magnificent under snow, but the prow of the Stuic is no place for walkers in winter.

Avoid it by ascending the west rim of Coire nan Eun, or ascend Lochnagar by the standard route from the Spittal of Glenmuick.

The vast tableland of the White Mounth ends abruptly in the north at the great granite peak of Lochnagar, which towers over the rivers and forests of Deeside. Artists and poets as well as climbers have long been attracted here to the dramatic scenery of the north-east corrie, a spectacular crescent of cliffs enclosing the dark lochan that gives the mountain its name. Although there are many routes to the summit, but by far the most interesting is by Ballochbuie Forest and the prow of The Stuic. This was the approach favoured by Lord Byron, whose atmospheric poem did much to further the fame of the mountain, with its stirring references to 'the steep frowning glories of dark Lochnagar'.

Begin at Invercauld Bridge where the A93 crosses the Dee 3 miles (5km) east of Braemar; parking is possible 150m further along in the Ballater direction, at the turn-off to Keiloch. Forest roads leave each side of the bridge to join on the south side of the old bridge and enter magnificent Ballochbuie Forest, purchased by Queen Victoria in 1878 to preserve it from felling and now the finest stand of pines in the Highlands.

At a fork after going 500m, take the right branch and then keep straight on at the next crossroads to join another track up the left bank (right side) of the Garbh Allt. Unlike modern forestry roads, these Victorian ones blend beautifully with the trees and make enchanting walking. At a hairpin bend, keep left on a path that passes close by the wild and mysterious

The map shows:
- Invercauld Bridge
- Ballochbuie Forest
- Garbh Allt
- Feindallacher Burn
- Gelder Shiel
- Sandy Loch
- Loch nan Eun
- CAC CARN BEAG 1155m / 3789'
- CAC CARN MOR 1150m / 3772'
- THE STUIC 1093m / 3585'
- CARN A' CHOIRE BOIDHEACH 1118m / 3667'
- MEIKLE PAP
- Lochnagar
- LOCHNAGAR
- kilometre
- mile

Falls of Garbh Allt before rejoining the forest road higher up. The road continues up the left bank (right side) of the Feindallacher Burn. When the trees begin to thin out, cut left across the burn and head across the rough heathery moor to the Allt Lochan nan Eun and Sandy Loch. The Stuic begins to look decidedly interesting from here, with its steep prow bisecting Coire nan Eun into two halves, each cradling lochans. Bear right into the corrie and climb the prow direct, a fine easy scramble on secure blocks of granite.

At the top, follow the path round the corrie rim (bagging the dreary Munro of Carn a' Coire Boidheach en route if you so desire) to Cac Carn Mor and Cac Carn Beag, the twin tops of Lochnagar. Both these tops lie on the rim of the north-east corrie, and as you stroll between

The north-east corrie of Lochnagar in winter.

them you should keep close to the edge to contemplate the vertiginous cliffs and the dark lochan far below. To descend, boulder hop down the north-west ridge of Cac Carn Beag to reach Sandy Loch and make your return via the approach route.

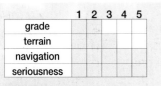

Route 41: BRAERIACH AND CAIRN TOUL • THE CAIRNGORMS

	1	2	3	4	5
grade					
terrain					
navigation					
seriousness					

OS MAP: 36
GR: 915087
DISTANCE: 22 miles (35km)
ASCENT: 1,580m (5,200ft)
TIME: 12½ hours

ASSESSMENT: probably the best high-level plateau walk in Scotland.

SEASONAL NOTES: the plateau and its corniced rims are spectacular in winter, but the complete route is a formidable undertaking that cannot be completed in daylight hours alone and is best attempted only in excellent conditions. Note that the exit from Coire Dhondail is very steep and may be corniced.

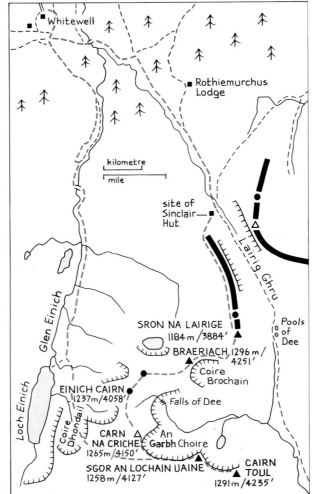

The Cairngorm plateau is the largest slice of high country in Britain, with over 200 square miles of land over 610m (2,000ft) and four of Scotland's five highest mountains. It is rugged Arctic-like country, unique in the Highlands, a massive primeval landscape whose exploration is at the same time both a fascinating experience and a serious undertaking. Its four 4,000ft (1,220m) peaks are divided into two groups by the deep trench of the Lairig Ghru, and three long routes are recommended for their exploration (Routes 41, 42 and 43).

The walk from the summit of Cairn Toul to the summit of Braeriach, the third and fourth highest peaks in the country, is perhaps the finest high-level plateau walk of all, not once dropping below 1,130m (3,700ft) during its 3½ mile (6km) circuit around the yawning depths of An Garbh Choire. Begin at Whitewell car park, at the end of the minor road that leaves the B970 south-east of Inverdruie. A signposted path goes down to join the Land Rover track along Gleann Einich, which is followed for 6 miles (10km) to the great ice-scoured basin where Loch Einich lies at the foot of the crags of Sgor Gaoith.

Just after the last bend before the loch, take the path on the left that rises across the hillside into the grassy hollow of Coire Dhondail and zigzags up the head of the corrie beside a fine waterslide to end on the plateau. From here make a rising traverse eastwards to the bealach below Sgor an Lochain Uaine, where massive An Garbh Choire comes into view, with its semi-permanent snow beds that have disappeared only twice this century. Follow the cliff edge over Sgor an Lochain Uaine (a new Munro in 1997, also known as Angel's Peak) and around Coire an Lochain Uaine to the summit of Cairn Toul, superbly situated at the apex of a number of high corries above the Lairig Ghru. Return to the bealach, leave the corrie rim, and follow the plateau skyline round to Braeriach, crossing a gravel desert that is a navigational test-piece in foul weather. Between Carn na Criche and Einich Cairn it is worth a short diversion right to the Wells of Dee, where a cairn marks the origin of that great river.

Reach the summit of Braeriach at the lip of the 230m (750ft) cliffs of Coire Bhrochain (meaning 'Porridge Corrie') and continue around the narrowing cliff edge on an indistinct path. The corrie is said to be named after the eventual consistency of some cattle that fell into it. At a dip, go left over the two tops of Sron na Lairige and down the rough north ridge. At the foot of the ridge a good path leads to the site of the former Sinclair Hut and the Lairig Ghru path, which provides a delightful descent through Rothiemurchus pine woods back to the Glen Einich track.

An Garbh Choire from Ben Macdui.

	1	2	3	4	5
grade					
terrain					
navigation					
seriousness					

OS MAP: 36/43
GR: 068898
DISTANCE: 19 miles (30km)
ASCENT: 1,020m (3,350ft)
TIME: 10 hours

ASSESSMENT: a long easy walk amidst constantly changing scenery that shows the many moods of the Cairngorm landscape.

SEASONAL NOTES: a fine but lengthy winter's day; the exposed summit plateau of Ben Macdui is best avoided in adverse weather.

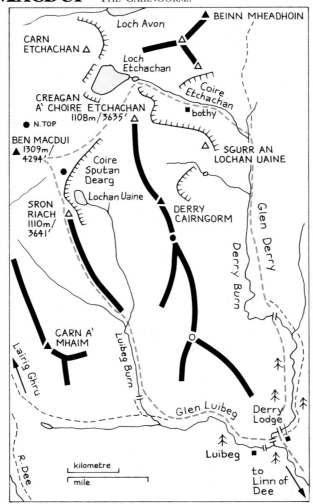

'For every few steps I took I heard a crunch, and then another crunch as if someone was walking after me but taking steps three or four times the length of my own. I said to myself 'This is all nonsense'. I listened and heard it again but could see nothing in the mist. As I walked on and the eerie crunch, crunch, sounded behind me I was seized with terror and took to my heels, staggering blindly among the boulders for four or five miles nearly down to Rothiemurchus Forest.'

PROFESSOR NORMAN COLLIE admitting in 1925 to an experience of 1891.

Ben Macdui is the second highest mountain in Scotland. Until well into the last century it was thought to be the highest, and this may account for the historical popularity of a mountain that lies well-hidden in the centre of the Cairngorms. Famous ascents include those by Gladstone, Queen Victoria (on a pony in 1859) and Professor Norman Collie, the celebrated mountaineer and one of many who have fled from the mountain before the legendary spectre of the Big Grey Man. It is certainly an eerie, desolate place and testaments to the Big Grey Man abound, but the undeterred walker will find its long, easy ascent a route of constant interest that shows the variegated Cairngorm landscape in all its many forms.

Begin at the foot of Glen Lui near the Linn of Dee west of Braemar. Take the rough road that crosses the broad flats beside the Lui Water (where large numbers of deer are often to be seen) to Derry Lodge in a fine situation at the junction of Glen Derry and Glen Luibeg. Cross the Derry Burn (footbridge) and take the Lairig an Laoigh path (signposted) through an enchanted forest of native pines to rejoin a Land Rover track from Derry Lodge further up Glen Derry.

The track becomes a path leading through the desolate upper glen below Coire an Lochan Uaine, a favourite haunt of the 18th-century Gaelic poet-cum-poacher, William Smith. At the head of the glen the path forks, the right branch continuing to Aviemore; take the left branch, which curves round into Coire Etchachan, a deep basin backed by crags and sporting a hut (the Hutchison Memorial Hut) that gives the place an Alpine flavour. Beyond the hut, the path climbs beside the burn to the corrie rim and debouches into an unexpected higher corrie filled by Loch Etchachan, the largest loch above the 3,000ft (914m) contour in the Highlands and frozen for much of the year. The scenery now becomes more Arctic than Alpine.

The path climbs left to the rim of Coire Sputan Dearg, yet another (and probably the finest) of Macdui's corries, and then veers right across the plateau to the summit boulderfield, strewn with stone howffs (shelters). Care should be taken in mist. Return to the rim of Coire Sputan Dearg and follow it down to the small top of Sron Riach, beneath whose crags sparkles lovely Lochan Uaine, evidence of why Macdui's collec-

tion of high lochans is said to be the finest in the Cairngorms. Continue down the south-east ridge of Sron Riach, picking up a path leading down to Glen Luibeg and the Lairig Ghru path, whose wide, sandy swathes provide a beautiful route through the pines back to Derry Lodge.

Coire Sputan Dearg, Ben Macdui, from Sron Riach.

	1	2	3	4	5
grade					
terrain					
navigation					
seriousness					

OS MAP: 36
GR: 983087
DISTANCE: 17 miles (27km)
ASCENT: 1,520m (5,000ft)
TIME: 10½ hours

ASSESSMENT: a wild walk around some secret corners of Cairn Gorm.

SEASONAL NOTES: a long and spectacular winter route, but the ascent from the Saddle and the descent into Coire an Lochan are very steep and not for the inexperienced. The summit plateau of Cairn Gorm is best avoided in adverse weather; the easiest descent from the summit goes northwards to the Ptarmigan Restaurant and down into Coire Cas.

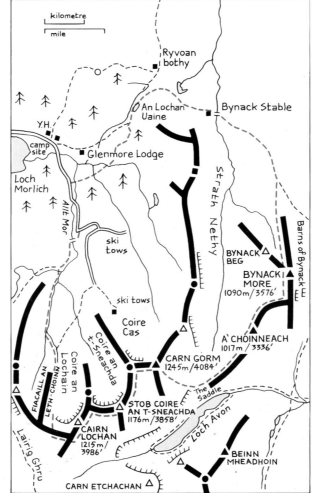

Prominent in all Speyside views, Cairn Gorm has given its name to the whole range of mountains that are more properly called the Monadh Ruadh (Red Mountains). Its wilderness nature has diminished somewhat in recent years as a result of downhill ski developments in its northern corries, and indeed the walker can now be chairlifted almost to the summit from the car park in Coire Cas. Yet Cairn Gorm is big enough still to contain in its environs some magnificent untouched corries, and a tour around some of these hidden haunts provides a magnificent route that avoids Coire Cas altogether.

Begin on the Cairn Gorm ski road east of Loch Morlich. Take the path that enters the forest on the left about 100m before a wide dirt road on the right. This path crosses the Allt Mor (bridge) and continues straight on (ignore all branches) to join the track from Glen More into the Pass of Ryvoan, a wonderfully Alpine pass with pines and crags overlooking the deep green eye of An Lochan Uaine. According to legend, the colour of the lochan, which has no visible outlet, derives from the fact that the fairies wash their clothes in it.

Keep right at a fork to reach the corrugated iron bothy of Bynack Stable at the foot of Strath Nethy. From here a finely graduated path crosses the shoulder of Bynack More into Glen Avon, providing an effortless climb to the foot of Bynack More's north ridge. Once onto the shoulder, leave the path and climb the ridge to the tumble of granite boulders that form the summit. Continue over A' Choinneach (which was classified as a Munro until 1981) to The Saddle, pausing on the way to explore the rocky tors of the Little Barns of Bynack. 'Nothing could be grander or wilder,' wrote Queen Victoria in 1861 of the tremendous view from The Saddle across wild Loch Avon, which rivals Loch Coruisk on Skye as the most remote loch in Britain.

From The Saddle, pick a route up the steep slopes rising 400m (1,300ft) to the broad, stony summit of Cairn Gorm, where the most spectacular section of the route begins, hugging the edge of the boulder-strewn plateau around the rims of Coire an t-Sneachda and Coire an Lochan. Note especially the huge walls of Coire an Lochan, the remote haunt of climbers far from the skiing areas (and may it ever remain so). Beneath the cliffs a glacier often forms in the spring, complete with crevasses, séracs and bergschrund.

Descend into the corrie on the path from the dip before Fiacaill an Leth-choin. If there is snow on the ground a direct descent here can be misleadingly steep, and it may be preferable to continue over the Fiacaill and descend further along. The path crosses the wild open moors below Coire an Lochan and eventually reaches a bridge over the Allt Mor to join the ski road not far above your starting point.

Winter climbing in Coire an Lochan.

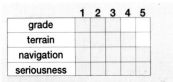

Route 44: BRUACH NA FRITHE (SKYE) •

	1	2	3	4	5
grade					
terrain					
navigation					
seriousness					

OS MAP: 32
GR: 480297
DISTANCE: 8½ miles (14km)
ASCENT: 990m (3,250ft)
TIME: 7 hours

ASSESSMENT: perhaps the best viewpoint and most easily reached summit on the Cuillin Ridge, but of no less character for all that and passing through some stunning rock scenery.

SEASONAL NOTES: although an easier winter ascent than many in the Cuillin, the steep corrie headwalls and narrow summit ridge may still provide major obstacles under snow.

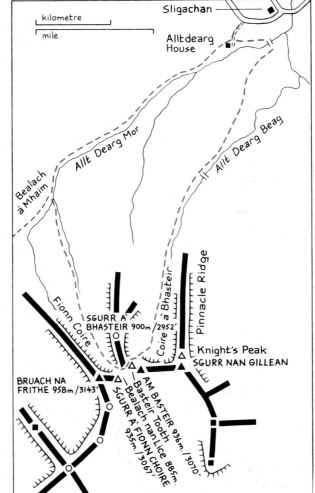

The meaning of the name 'Cuillin' remains obscure; possibilities include 'High Rocks' (from the Norse *Kjölen*), 'Holly' (from the Gaelic *Cuilion*, referring to the serrated skyline), 'Worthless' (from the Celtic, referring to the Cuillin's agricultural potential) and after Prince Cuchullin of Antrim.

Few mountain ranges attract as much devotion as the Cuillin of Skye. There is something about the nature of the rough gabbro peaks – the ambience of their setting above the blue expanse of the Sea of the Hebrides and the quality of the light suffusing them, that attracts the visitor again and again. For scramblers they are a delight: for 7 miles (11km) between Glen Sligachan and Glen Brittle the main Cuillin ridge presents a twisting arête of naked rock, sharp and pinnacled, hollowed out by idyllic corries, never dipping below 2,500ft (760m) and containing 14 peaks over 3,000ft (914m).

Many sections of the ridge are the preserve of the rock climber, and in adverse weather the compass-deflecting properties of the rock and the complexity of the rock architecture should deter the uninitiated from venturing high. But on a fine summer's day there is nothing to match the magic of the Cuillin, and the five routes recommended in this book (routes 44 – 48, in order of increasing difficulty) will provide memories for a lifetime.

Perhaps the easiest route in the Cuillin is the ascent of Bruach na Frithe. Begin 700m from Sligachan Hotel on the A863 Dunvegan road (car park) and take the path past Alltdearg

House up the left bank (right side) of the Allt Dearg Mor. At the confluence with the burn coming down from Fionn Coire, branch left at a large cairn and follow a path up the right bank (left side) of the burn into this untypically grassy but charming Cuillin corrie, with its attractive shelf of small lochans. Above the corrie the path climbs slopes of boulders and scree to reach the main ridge at the Bealach nan Lice, from where an easy traverse path leads around the rock bastion of Sgurr a' Fionn Choire and up Bruach na Frithe's stony east ridge to the summit.

On return to the Bealach nan Lice, wander out along the south ridge of Sgurr a' Bhasteir immediately beyond to study Pinnacle Ridge of Sgurr nan Gillean and the spectacular Basteir Tooth below Am Basteir. The easiest descent route is to reverse the ascent, but for a variation with slightly more scrambling, descend scree slopes from the main ridge into secluded Coire a' Bhasteir. Once into the corrie, pick up a cairned route to the left of and well above the rocky gorge of the Allt Dearg Beag; this leads out of the corrie and passes some idyllic pools on its way back across the moor to Sligachan.

For those who enjoy easy (if reasonably exposed) scrambling, ascend by the narrow shattered north-west ridge of Bruach na Frithe to the right of Fionn Coire.

Am Basteir, Sgurr nan Gillean and Sgurr a' Fhionn Choire from Bruach na Frithe.

Route 45: Sgurr Dearg (Skye) • The Islands: Skye

	1	2	3	4	5
grade					
terrain					
navigation					
seriousness					

OS MAP: 32
GR: 414205
DISTANCE: 5 miles (8km)
ASCENT: 990m (3,250ft)
TIME: 6 hours

ASSESSMENT: an essentially straightforward scramble rendered exciting by dramatic surroundings.

SEASONAL NOTES: the environs of the In Pin are no place for inexperienced mountaineers in winter.

'Inaccessible as it looks, this pinnacle may be surmounted by experienced climbers who love to do what no-one else has done and to boast thereof for ever after.'

*J A MACCULLOCH on the
Inaccessible Pinnacle
(The Misty Isle of Skye, 1905)*

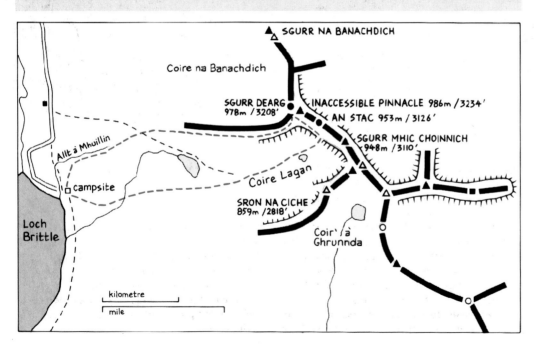

The round of Coire Lagan is a long-standing scrambler's test piece. It develops into what is technically a rock climb, but the ascent of Sgurr Dearg, which begins the round, has no great difficulty, providing a route through perhaps the most spectacular situations in a mountain range full of spectacular situations.

From Glen Brittle campsite take the path that begins behind the toilet block and makes a rising traverse left across the moor to the Allt a' Mhuillin. The path follows this stream, crosses another path and climbs to a conspicuous cairn-shaped boulder at the foot of the southwest shoulder of Sgurr Dearg. The well-trodden route up the shoulder begins steeply and then eases off to reach a narrow section of ridge just below the summit, where easy (slightly exposed) scrambling is required.

There can be few more dramatic mountain tops than the sharp summit crest of Sgurr Dearg, for even higher looms the preposterous blade of rock known as the Inaccessible Pinnacle, the only Munro that requires a rock climb for its ascent. Its very presence is enough to give some people vertigo. The route onwards

descends rough ground to the neck of rock between Sgurr Dearg and the 'In Pin', with vertiginous drops left to Coruisk, and contours to the right around the base of the pinnacle to the foot of its east ridge. Many backsides of breeches have been worn out here.

From the foot of the east ridge a short detour (an easy scramble) can be made out to the summit of An Stac for the best view of the In Pin, otherwise continue down the broad undercut ramp that traverses beneath the crest of An Stac. Take care to continue left around a corner (cairn), rather than right down some tempting scree that leads to crags, to regain the crest of the ridge at the Bealach Coire Lagan.

The scramble up Sgurr Mhic Choinnich, the next peak on the ridge, along perhaps the sharpest crest in the Cuillin, can be explored by those who are not of a nervous disposition, but most hillwalkers will be more than satisfied with what they have achieved already. From the Bealach Coire Lagan, descend scree slopes (An Stac screes) to the heart of Coire Lagan and pause beside the lochan to admire the scale of

Sgurr Dearg (left) and Coire Lagan from Glen Brittle.

your surroundings. The path down to Glen Brittle descends from the right-hand corner of the lochan beside boiler plate slabs, which lounge at the water's edge like enormous hippopotami. It is a pleasant descent across the moor, with the climber's playground of Sron na Ciche cliffs to your left and in front of you the endless sea.

Route 46: THE SOUTH CUILLIN RIDGE (SKYE) •

	1	2	3	4	5
grade					
terrain					
navigation					
seriousness					

OS MAP: 32
GR: 414205
DISTANCE: 9½ miles (15km)
ASCENT: 1,560m (5,100ft)
TIME: 10 hours

ASSESSMENT: a long and magnificent scramble of ceaseless interest amidst unearthly rock scenery and hypnotic seaward views. (The scrambles up to the Cioch and up Sgurr Alasdair are Grade 5)

especially around Sgurr Alasdair, require winter mountaineering skills.

SEASONAL NOTES: all sections of the main ridge,

There are few routes in Scotland that offer the mountain walker as much constant interest, satisfaction and exhilaration as the South Cuillin Ridge. Begin at Glen Brittle campsite and take the path behind the toilet block that climbs onto the moor and veers right to reach a stream at a small gorge. Cross the stream, turn immediately left along the far bank and follow a path that climbs diagonally around Sron na Ciche into lower Coir' a' Ghrunnda. The path keeps high above the Allt Coir' a' Ghrunnda, but you may wish to explore the fantastic boiler plate slabs in the centre of the corrie. The skyline in front of you is the lip of the upper corrie, behind which lies one of those idyllic Cuillin lochans whose beckoning waters on a hot day end many a stirring plan. As you approach the lip there are one or two passages of easy scrambling that may be awkward when wet.

The most enjoyable route up to the main Cuillin ridge scrambles up a staircase of huge boulders to the left of the rock bastion of An Caisteal behind the lochan. The rock here is so sharp, pitted and adhesive that the climbing potential of the Cuillin will soon become painfully obvious. The ridge is reached through a rock window, beyond which a path leads around the far side of An Caisteal to the north ridge of Sgurr nan Eag. Take the path on the right or scramble up the crest to reach the summit of Sgurr nan Eag, which is the third of three tors. A steep descent (optional scrambling) and re-ascent lead on across the narrow, shattered quartzite top of Sgurr a' Choire Bhig, and then a wonderfully airy ridge walk leads out to Gars-bheinn at the end of the main ridge.

To vary the return route from Gars-bheinn, continue around Coir' a' Ghrunnda, behind An Caisteal once more, and contour beneath the crags of Sgurr Alasdair to Bealach Coir' a' Ghrunnda. En route you may wish to climb Sgurr Dubh na Da Bheinn and Sgurr Dubh Mor. From the bealach there are two exciting routes down to Coire Lagan and Glen Brittle. The shortest and easiest descends the Sgumain Stone Shoot from the bealach beneath the awesome cliffs of Sron na Ciche. On descent, pause at a jumble of huge boulders to view the famous Cioch (an improbable knob of rock, which can be reached by a hard scramble left up a sloping terrace).

Perhaps even more rewarding, however, is the traverse of Sgurr Alasdair, from the foot of whose east ridge the renowned Alasdair Stone Shoot can be descended into Coire Lagan. This alternative involves much harder scrambling and route-finding, especially at the Bad Step just above the start of the ascent to Sgurr Alasdair (which can be bypassed on the right, using a small chimney), but what better way to end a magnificent day than atop the Cuillin's highest peak?

On the summit ridge of Sgurr nan Eag above Coir a' Ghrunnda.

	1	2	3	4	5
grade					
terrain					
navigation					
seriousness					

OS MAP: 32
GR: 409225
DISTANCE: 6 miles (10km)
ASCENT: 1,340m (4,400ft)
TIME: 8½ hours

ASSESSMENT: a long, sensational and continuously hard scramble with some memorable situations.

SEASONAL NOTES: the whole corrie skyline presents major mountaineering obstacles in winter.

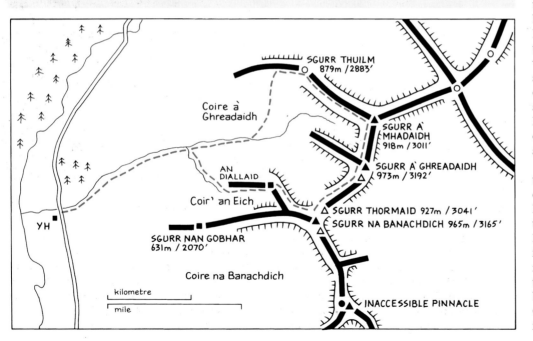

Coire a' Ghreadaidh is more open and might at first glance appear less dramatic than many Cuillin corries, but its beautiful pools and waterslides can be irresistibly inviting on a hot day. Moreover, the three massive Munros that form the corrie headwall, and the two long enclosing side ridges that project westwards to Sgurr Thuilm and Sgurr nan Gobhar, provide a high-level scramble around the corrie skyline that is both long and exciting.

Begin at Glen Brittle Youth Hostel and take the path up the left bank (right side) of the tumbling burn. Avoid a right branch to Sgurr na Banachdich and continue beside the burn into the flat bowl of the corrie and the picturesque waterslides at its back. If you can tear yourself away from this spot, cross the burn and climb directly up steep, tedious slopes of grass and scree to gain the summit ridge of Sgurr Thuilm. From the summit, descend the gentle southeast ridge to where it abuts sharply against the side of Sgurr a' Mhadaidh.

The scramble up Sgurr a' Mhadaidh attacks the left of two rock ribs and is hard and exposed; the easiest lines are on the the right. Higher up, a cairn marks the start of a path that traverses right to avoid the summit crags. If it all becomes too much, redescend to the foot of the scramble and traverse well to the right beneath the cliffs of Sgurr a' Mhadaidh to the prominent scree gully (An Dorus) between Sgurr a' Mhadaidh and Sgurr a' Ghreadaidh, and scramble easily to the summit from there.

Continuing around the corrie beyond An Dorus, hard scrambling remains the order of the day as you climb past Eag Dubh (the Black Cleft) and the rock bastion known as the Wart, to reach the summit of Sgurr a' Ghreadaidh. Then the ridge narrows to a spectacular knife-edge and crosses a southern top before descending to a bealach. Impressive looking Sgurr Thormaid, with its three 'teeth', now rears ahead, but the scrambling is easier than what you have already done; the easiest line keeps to the left on the way up and to the right on the descent of the far side. The final ascent of the day up Sgurr na Banachdich is easy, providing you avoid the crags on the left.

To descend, go down Sgurr na Banachdich's stony western slopes to a small plateau at the start of the narrowing ridge leading out to

Sgurr a' Ghreadaidh from Sgurr na Banachdich.

Sgurr nan Gobhar, and from here follow a path down the spur ridge of An Diallaid to regain the corrie. Alternatively, to prolong the scrambling, continue out to the grass-topped sentinel of Sgurr nan Gobhar above Glen Brittle and descend the steep gully between the peak's two tops.

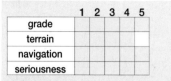

	1	2	3	4	5
grade					
terrain					
navigation					
seriousness					

OS MAP: 32
GR: 485298
DISTANCE: 7 miles (11km)
ASCENT: 1,010m (3,300ft)
TIME: 6½ hours

ASSESSMENT: the route is straightforward except for a hard and exposed final scramble, but it is well worth the attempt for the fine situations of the approach.

SEASONAL NOTES: the final scramble will be beyond the capabilities of most non-climbers when iced or under snow.

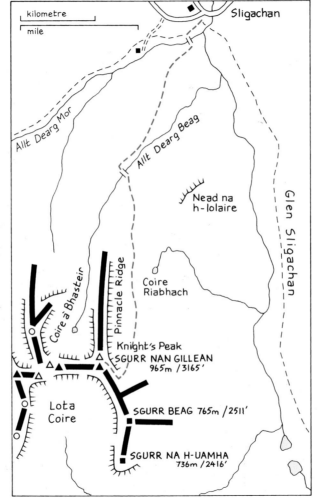

The Cuillin remained unclimbed until the physicist and geologist Professor James Forbes persuaded Duncan MacIntyre, a local forester, to guide him up Sgurr nan Gillean on 7th July 1836. The route they pioneered has since become known as the Tourist Route.

No one could fail to be thrilled by the first view of the Cuillin from Sligachan – the great rock peaks soaring high above the moorland, and with the steep tapering cone of Sgurr nan Gillean prominent to the left. For the non-climber, the only feasible route to the summit of Sgurr nan Gillean is the misleadingly named Tourist Route, and even this is a hard and exposed scramble in its final stages. The ascent has much to recommend it, however, even if you decide it would be best to leave the last few metres for another day.

Begin opposite Sligachan Hotel and take the path along the left bank (right side) of the Allt Dearg Mor. Branch left across the river after a few hundred metres (bridge) to follow another path across the almost flat moor to the Allt Dearg Beag, whose beautiful pools and water cascades are followed to another fork at another bridge. Cross the bridge and follow the left branching path across the broad, flat ridge above Nead na h-Iolaire and into the heathery Coire Riabhach.

Keeping well above the lochan in the bowl of the corrie, the path climbs steep, stony slopes around Sgurr nan Gillean's east face and reaches a higher, smaller corrie whose floor is a chaotic jumble of boulders. The path becomes indistinct in places but it is well cairned; it continues up the gully at the back of the corrie and reaches the skyline at the south-east ridge.

Now the excitement begins as the airy crest of the ridge is followed up to the summit platform. There are many route options at first, but as the steepening summit cone gets nearer, the scrambling becomes harder and more exposed. On the last 30m (100ft) there are only two possible routes: the extremely narrow crest of the ridge or sloping rocks to the left; remember that you will have to reverse the moves on descent. Should you decide in your wisdom that the summit is best left to impoverished Munro baggers, console yourself with the knowledge that Sgurr nan Gillean was considered unclimbable until its first ascent in 1836.

Unless you decide to take up permanent residence at the summit, there is but one route off for hillwalkers – the way you came up, but if you wish to prolong the scrambling, the two smaller peaks of Sgurr Beag and Sgurr na h-Uamha south of Sgurr nan Gillean are worth a closer look once you are down the south-east ridge. Sgurr na h-Uamha in particular is a fine little mountain, whose exciting ascent is of a similar standard to the final section of the Tourist Route but, again, remember that you will have to reverse the moves on the way down.

Sgurr nan Gillean from Sligachan.

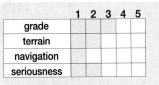

	1	2	3	4	5
grade					
terrain					
navigation					
seriousness					

OS MAP: 32
GR: 545172
DISTANCE: 8 miles (13km)
ASCENT: 1,100m (3,600ft)
TIME: 6½ hours

ASSESSMENT: an untypically easy ascent with typically superb views on a Cuillin outlier.

SEASONAL NOTES: in rare winter conditions this route remains probably the only easy Cuillin ascent, at least as far as the south top.

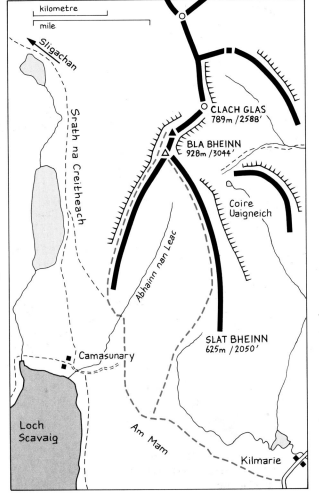

'And over all broods the mighty mass of Blaaven, gleaming with rich purple, its clefts white with dazzling snow-wreaths, and wisps of cloud stealing around its secret top. It is a mountain among mountains, a king among them all, whose magic influence fills the heart...'

J A MACCULLOCH
(The Misty Isle of Skye, 1905)

Bla Bheinn is separated from the main Cuillin ridge by the deep trough of Srath na Creitheach. When climbed in conjunction with the main ridge it forms the Greater Cuillin Traverse, a major test of mountaineering skill and fitness involving over 4,000m (13,000ft) of ascent. Alexander Nicolson, that renowned pioneer explorer of the Cuillin, considered Bla Bheinn the finest mountain in Skye. It exhibits all the character of a typical Cuillin peak, and in addition gains from its isolation, offering superb views of the main ridge. The complete traverse of Bla Bheinn, and its neighbouring rock tower Clach Glas, is Alpine in nature and is no place for walkers, but the south ridge provides a unique Cuillin ascent that, in the famous words of an early guidebook, is 'delightfully easy'.

The route to the foot of the south ridge begins on the A881 Broadford–Elgol road 400m south of Kilmarie, from where a Land Rover track crosses the shallow bealach of Am Mam (The Moor) south of Bla Bheinn to Camasunary on Loch Scavaig. At Am Mam the sharp crest of the south ridge comes into view for the first time, rising evenly and invitingly from seashore to mountain top. Twenty metres before the hairpin bend on the descent to Camasunary (cairn), branch right on a path that cuts across the hillside and crosses the Abhainn nan Leac to the foot of the south ridge. Leave the path a couple of hundred metres beyond the stream, at a large cairn on a boulder, and take the path that climbs the ridge.

Initial steep grass slopes lead to a craggy brow (bypassed on the right) and the increasingly rocky upper ridge, where scrambling of all grades can be sought – or avoided almost altogether – by keeping to the path. The ridge eventually debouches onto the stony dome of the south top. The higher north top lies 200m away across a short dip, whose negotiation requires some handwork. The easiest route descends a steep earth gully to just below the dip. A more direct and interesting route involves an easy if slightly exposed scramble along a ledge on the left near the top of this gully. The view from the two tops across Srath na Creitheach to the Cuillin is superb.

In fine weather a return via the lochan-studded plateau of Slat Bheinn makes a delightful contrast to the ascent route. From the south top descend the steep, stony south-eastern slopes of the mountain that rim Coire Uaigneich; in places there is an indistinct path. From the small lochan at the foot of the slope a pleasant stroll across the plateau

leads back to Am Mam and the Land Rover track which will take you back to your starting point at Kilmarie.

Bla Bheinn from the Red Hills.

	1	2	3	4	5
grade					
terrain					
navigation					
seriousness					

OS MAP: 23
STARTING POINT: Storr Forest
(GR: 511531)
ROUTE TYPE: return hill walk
DISTANCE: 3½ miles (6km)
ASCENT: 550m (1,800ft)
TIME: 4+ hours

ASSESSMENT: a visit to the weird rock pinnacles of the highest mountain in north Skye, followed by an ascent to its summit above disintegrating cliffs.

CLIMBING NOTE: *'The Old Man may be climbable but we didn't make an attempt.'* Victorian climber Harold Raeburn's famous throwaway remark, expressing an understandable reluctance to rope up. Don Whillans made the first ascent of the Old Man in 1955; the route is graded Very Severe and begins on the north-west face near the right-hand end of the overhang.

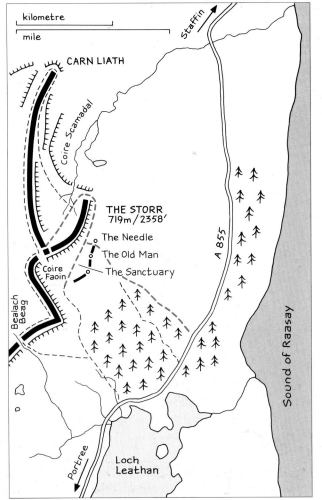

It is at the Storr that the backbone of the Trotternish peninsula begins to erupt into the contorted forms for which it is renowned. The view of the Storr from the coast road north of Portree must be one of the most famous and photographed on Skye, with the summit cliffs of the mountain given scale by the Old Man at their foot. The Old Man is only one of a number of extraordinary pinnacles that ring the basin known as the Sanctuary, and the walk up to the Sanctuary is one of the most popular excursions on Skye.

The path through the Storr forest to the Sanctuary from the car park at the foot of the Storr is seriously boggy and is best avoided until it has been improved. Alternative paths climb each side of the forest; the easiest route up at the time of writing follows the fence on the north side. The array of pinnacles that guard the secluded interior of the Sanctuary give it the aura of a prehistoric site, and you will want to spend some time exploring here. The famous Old Man in particular is like a megalithic stone. It teeters 50m (165ft) above its plinth and is undercut all around; the rock is so flaky that it comes away in your fingers. Nearby is the improbable Needle, a fragile wedge of rock with two 'eyes' left by fallen blocks.

Behind the Sanctuary tower the 200m (650ft) rotten summit cliffs of the Storr, split into five buttresses by deep dark gullies. The route to the summit follows a path around the foot of the cliffs on the right (north) to gain the north-east corrie above the crags of Coire Scamadal. A line of cairns then points the way up to a V-shaped nick in the skyline, where a grassy gully breaches the cliffs (a short section of handwork is required here) to deposit you on the summit plateau not far from the trig. point.

The quickest route down is the route of ascent, but detours either northwards or southwards along the plateau can be used to add variety to the descent. The southward detour follows the plateau rim down to the Bealach Beag, then descends the left bank of the stream from here (another short section of handwork required) and crosses the moor to the south side of the Storr Forest. The northward detour follows the north ridge to the castellated rocky eminence of Carn Liath. The impressive northern cliffs of Carn Liath, hidden on approach, sport the cleanest climbing rock on the Storr, and beneath them is perhaps the most chaotic terrain in all Trotternish. The rarely visited summit is gained by an easy scramble on the south side.

Pinnacles of the Sanctuary; the Old Man is in the middle.

GLOSSARY/INDEX

Note: entries are indexed by route number, not page.